Archangels
Don't Play Pinball

DARIO FO was born in 1926 in Lombardy. He began working in the theatre in 1951 as a comic and mime. Together with his wife, Franca Rame, he was highly successful as actor, director and writer of satirical comedies for the conventional theatre. In the Sixties they abandoned it; Fo began to write for a wider audience in factories and workers' clubs and produced work which was not only an important political intervention in Italy but has been internationally acclaimed. In 1970 he and his wife founded the theatrical collective, La Comune, in Milan. His work – and the work of Franca Rame – has been performed in England with great success: *Can't Pay? Won't Pay!* (Half Moon Theatre and Criterion Theatre, London, 1981); *Accidental Death of an Anarchist* (Half Moon Theatre and Wyndham's Theatre, London, 1980); *Female Parts* by Franca Rame (National Theatre, London, 1981); *Mistero Buffo* (Riverside Theatre, London, 1983); *Trumpets and Raspberries* (Palace Theatre, Watford; Phoenix Theatre, London, 1984); *Archangels Don't Play Pinball* (Bristol Old Vic, 1986) and *Elizabeth* (Half Moon Theatre, London, 1986).

The front cover shows Roger Rees as Lofty *and Simon Slater as the* Conjuror *in the 1986 production of* Archangels Don't Play Pinball *at the Bristol Old Vic. The photograph is reproduced by courtesy of Allen Daniels. The back cover photograph is of Dario Fo and is reproduced by courtesy of Max Whitaker.*

Also by Dario Fo

Accidental Death of an Anarchist
Can't Pay? Won't Pay!
Elizabeth
Female Parts (co-author: Franca Rame)
Trumpets and Raspberries

Series editor: Stuart Hood

Dario Fo

Archangels Don't Play Pinball

Translated by R.C. McAVOY and A-M. GIUGNI
Introduced by STUART HOOD

A Methuen Paperback

A METHUEN MODERN PLAY

This translation first published in Great Britain in 1987 as a
paperback original by Methuen London Ltd.,
11 New Fetter Lane, London EC4P 4EE.

Original Italian edition copyright © Dario Fo 1959
Translation copyright © R.C. McAvoy and A-M. Giugni 1987
Introduction copyright © Methuen London 1987.

Set in Times Roman by Theatretexts,
Waterguard House, 1 Branch Road, London E.14
Printed in Great Britain

British Library Cataloguing in Publication Data

Fo, Dario
    Archangels don't play pinball.—(Methuen
    modern plays)
    I. Title II. Hood, Stuart III. Gli arcangeli
    non giocano al flipper. *English*
    852'.914 PQ4866.02

    ISBN 0   413   15630   3

Contents

INTRODUCTION
The Theatre of Dario Fo and Franca Rame

The son of a railway worker, Dario Fo was born in 1926 near
the Lago Maggiore in Northern Italy. He grew up in a village
community that included glass-blowers and smugglers, where
there was a strong tradition of popular narrative – much of it
humorously subversive of authority – fed by travelling
story-tellers and puppeteers. Gifted artistically, he studied
architecture at Milan at the art-school attached to the Brera
Gallery; but the theatre drew him strongly – first as a
set-designer and then as a performer. His career began in
revue which was the spectacular escapist entertainment of
post-war Italy with girls and comics (some very brilliant like
Totò, whom Fo greatly admired) and glamorous *chanteuses*. It
was a genre favoured by politicians of the ruling Christian
Democrat party; girls' legs were preferable to the social
preoccupations of contemporary Italian cinema. In revue Fo
began to make his mark as an extraordinarily original comic
and mime. On radio he built a reputation with his monologues
as Poer Nano – the poor simpleton who, in telling Bible
stories, for example, gets things wrong, preferring Cain to the
insufferable prig, Abel. In 1954 he married Franca Rame, a
striking and talented actress, who came from a family of
travelling players and had made her first stage appearance
when she was eight days old. Together they embarked on a
highly successful series of productions.

In the fifties the right-wing clerical Christian Democrat
government had imposed a tight censorship on film, theatre
and broadcasting. Fo took advantage of a slight relaxation in

censorship to mount an 'anti-revue', *Il dito nell'occhio* (One in the Eye). His aim was clear – to attack those myths in Italian life which, as he said, 'Fascism had imposed and Christian Democracy had preserved.' *Il dito nell'occhio* was 'one in the eye' for official versions of history. Presented at the Piccolo Teatro in Milan it was an immense success to which the participation of the great French mime, Jacques Lecoq, from whom Fo learned much, was an important contribution. *Il dito nell'occhio* was the first in a series of pieces which drew on French farce, on the traditional sketches of the Rame family, and on the traditions of the circus. This mixture of spectacle, mime and social comment was highly successful but made the authorities nervous; the police were frequently present at performances, following the scripts with pocket torches to ensure that there were no departures from the officially approved text. Fo grew in stature and virtuosity as actor and comic, exploiting his extraordinary range of gesture, movement and facial expression, his variety of voices and accents, and his skill as a story-teller. It was the misfortune of Italian cinema that it was unable to exploit his talents. There were difficulties in finding suitable scripts and, on set, his vitality and spontaneity were denied the space and freedom that the theatre provided. But what Fo did take away from film was an understanding of how montage gave pace to narrative.

In 1959 the Dario Fo–Franca Rame company was invited to open a season at the Odeon Theatre in Milan. The piece they chose was *Gli arcangeli non giocano a flipper* (Archangels Don't Play Pinball), written, directed and designed by Fo. It was unusual in that it dealt critically with certain ludicrous aspects of Italian society. The middle-class audience were astonished by its rhythms and technique and delighted by Fo in the leading role – that of a wise simpleton, who looks back to Poer Nano and forward to a series of similar clowns in later work. Fo and Rame were now securely established both as actors and as personalities in the public eye. Their success in conventional theatre was confirmed by a series of pieces which exploited a mixture of comedy, music and farcical plots in which Fo would, for instance, double as an absent-minded priest and a bandit. The social references were there – Fo and Rame were now both close to the Communist Party and acutely aware of the political tensions in society – and the public readily picked them up. In a period which saw widespread industrial unrest culminating in the general strike of 1960 their material caused the authorities in Milan to threaten to ban performances.

Italian television had been for many years a fief of the Christian Democrats. Programme control was strict: a young woman given to wearing tight sweaters who looked like winning a popular quiz show had to be eliminated on moral grounds. But when in 1962 the centre-left of the Christian Democrats became dominant there was some relaxation of censorship. It was in these circumstances that the Fo–Rame team was invited to appear on the most popular TV show, *Canzonissima*, which, as its name suggests, featured heart-throb singers along with variety acts. Into this show the Fo's proceeded to inject their own brand of subversive humour – such as a sketch in which a worker whose aunt has fallen into a mincing-machine, which cannot be stopped for that would interrupt production, piously takes her home as tinned meat. The reaction of the political authorities and of the right-wing press was to call for censorship, duly imposed by the obedient functionaries of Italian television – all of them political appointees. There was a tussle of wills at the end of which the Fo's walked out of the show. The scandal was immense. There were parliamentary questions; threats of law-suits on both sides. Fo had public opinion solidly behind him. He had, he said, tried to look behind the facade of the 'economic miracle', to question the view that 'we were all one big family now' and to show how exploitation had increased and scandals flourished. By subverting *Canzonissima* from within he had established himself with a huge popular audience.

During this period Fo had become interested in material set in or drawn from the Middle Ages. He had begun 'to look at the present with the instruments of history and culture in order to judge it better'. He invited the public to use these instruments by writing an ambitious piece, *Isabella, tre*

caravelle e un cacciaballe (Isabella, Three Caravels and a
Wild-Goose Chaser), in which Columbus – that schoolbook
hero – is portrayed as the upwards striving intellectual who
loses out in the game of high politics. It was a period when
Brecht's *Galileo* was playing with great success in Milan and
the theatre was a subject of intense debate in the intellectual
and political ferment leading up to the unrest of 1968. For Fo
the most important result was probably his collaboration with
a group of left-wing musicians who had become interested in
the political potential of popular songs. Their work appealed
to him because he was himself 'interested above all in a past
attached to the roots of the people... and the concept of "the
new in the traditional".' They put together a show, built round
popular and radical songs, to which Fo contributed his
theories on the importance of gesture and the rhythms in the
performance of folksong; it marked an important step in his
development.

In 1967 he put on his last production for the bourgeois
theatre, *La signora non è da buttare* (The Lady's Not For
Discarding), in which a circus was made the vehicle for an
attack on the United States and capitalist society in general. It
again attracted the attention of the authorities. Fo was called
to police headquarters in Milan and threatened with arrest for
'offensive lines', not included in the approved version,
attacking a head of state – Lyndon Johnson. By now it was
becoming 'more and more difficult to act in a theatre where
everything down to the subdivision of the seating... mirrored
the class divisions. The choice for an intellectual', Fo
concluded, 'was to leave his gilded ghetto and put himself at
the disposal of the movement.'

The company with which the Fo's confronted this task was
the cooperative Nuova Scena – an attempt to dispense with
the traditional roles in a stage company and to make
decision-making collective. It was, Fo said in retrospect, a
utopian project in which individual talents and capabilities
were sacrificed to egalitarian principles. But whatever the
internal difficulties there was no doubt as to the success the
company enjoyed with a new public which it sought out in the

working-class estates, in cooperatives and trade union halls, in factories and workers' clubs. It was a public which knew nothing of the theatre but which found the political attitudes the company presented close to its experience of life. Each performance was followed by a discussion.

Nuova Scena did not last long – it was torn apart by political arguments, by arguments over the relationship of art to society and politics, and by questions of organisation. There were also difficulties with the Communist Party, which often controlled the premises used and whose officials began to react negatively to satirical attacks on their bureaucracy, the inflexibility of the Party line, the intolerance of real discussion. Before the split came, the company had put on a *Grande pantomima con bandiere e pupazzi medi e piccoli* (Grand Pantomime with Flags and Little and Medium Puppets), in which Fo used a huge puppet, drawn from the Sicilian tradition, to represent the state and its continual fight with the 'dragon' of the working class. But the most important production was Fo's one-man show *Mistero Buffo*, which was to become one of his enduring triumphs in Italy and abroad. In it he drew on the counter-culture of the Middle Ages, on apocryphal gospel stories, on legend and tales, presenting episodes in which he played all the roles and used a language in part invented, in part archaic, in part drawn from the dialects of Northern Italy. It has been described as 'an imaginary Esperanto of the poor and disinherited'. In performing the scenes of which *Mistero Buffo* is composed – such as the resurrection of Lazarus, the marriage at Cana, Pope Boniface's encounter with Jesus on the Via Dolorosa and others – Fo drew on two main traditions: that of the *giullare* (inadequately translated into English as 'jester'), the travelling comic, singer, mime, who in the Middle Ages was the carrier of a subversive culture; and that of the great clowns of the Commedia dell'Arte with their use of masks, of dialect and of *grammelot*, that extraordinary onomatopoeic rendering of a language – French, say – invented by the 15th-century comedians in which there are accurate sounds and intonations but few real words, all adding up (with the aid of highly expressive mime) to intelligible discourse.

When Nuova Scena split in 1970 it came hard on the heels of mounting polemics in the Communist press. Looking back, Franca Rame has admitted that she and Dario Fo were perhaps sectarian and sometimes mistaken but that they had had to break with the Communist cultural organisations if they wished to progress. The result was La Comune, a theatre company with its headquarters in Milan. The Fo's were now politically linked to the new Left, which found the Communist Party too authoritarian, too locked in the mythology of the Resistance, too inflexible and increasingly conservative. In *Morte accidentale di un'anarchico* (Accidental Death of an Anarchist) Fo produced a piece in which his skill at writing farce and his gifts as a clown were put brilliantly at the service of his politics, playing on the tension between the real death of a prisoner and the farcical inventions advanced by the authorities to explain it. It is estimated that in four years the piece was seen by a million people, many of whom took part in fierce debates after the performance. Fo had succeeded in his aim of making of the theatre 'a great machine which makes people laugh at dramatic things... In the laughter there remains a sediment of anger.' So no easy catharsis. There followed a period in which Fo was deeply engaged politically – both through his writings and through his involvement with Franca Rame, who was the main mover of the project – in Red Aid, which collected funds and comforts for Italian political prisoners detained in harsh conditions. His writing dealt with the Palestinian struggle, with Chile, with the methods of the Italian police. In the spring of 1973 Franca Rame was kidnapped from her home in Milan by a Fascist gang, gravely assaulted and left bleeding in the street. Fo himself later that year was arrested and held in prison in Sardinia for refusing to allow police to be present at rehearsals. Demonstrations and protests ensured his release. Dario Fo had, as his lawyer said, for years no longer been only an actor but a political figure whom the state powers would use any weapon to silence.

His political flair was evident in the farce *Non si paga, non si paga* (Can't Pay? Won't Pay!) dating from 1974, which deals with the question of civil disobedience. Significantly, the main upholder of law and order is a Communist shop steward, who disapproves of his wife's gesture of rebellion against the rising cost of living – a raid on a supermarket. It was a piece tried out on and altered at the suggestion of popular audiences – a practice Fo has often used. It was the same spirit that inspired his *Storia di una tigre* (Story of a Tiger), an allegorical monologue dating from 1980 – after a trip to China, and based on a Chinese folktale – the moral of which is that, if you have 'tiger' in you, you must never delegate responsibility to others, never expect others to solve your own problems, and above all avoid that unthinking party loyalty which is the enemy of reason and of revolution. In 1981, following on the kidnapping of Aldo Moro came *Clacson, trombette e pernacchi* (Trumpets and Raspberries). In it Fo doubled as Agnelli, the boss of FIAT, and a FIAT shop steward, whose identities become farcically confused. The play mocks the police and their readiness to see terrorists everywhere and the political cynicism which led to Moro's being abandoned to his fate by his fellow-politicians.

It was the last of Fo's major political works to date. Looking for new fields at a time when the great political upsurge has died away and the consumerist state has apparently triumphed, Fo has turned in recent years to a play on Elizabeth and Essex, with a splendid transvestite part for himself which allows him to use the dialect of *Mistero Buffo*, and a Harlequinade – a slight but charming piece that returns to the techniques of the Commedia dell'Arte.

Meanwhile Franca Rame, who has progressively established herself as a political figure and a powerful feminist, has produced a number of one-woman plays, partly in collaboration with her husband – monologues which are a direct political intervention in a society where the role of women is notably restricted by the Church, the state and male traditions. Like all their work the one-woman plays such as *Il risveglio* (Waking Up) or *Una donna sola* (A Woman Alone) depend on the tension between the unbearable nature of the situation in which the female protagonist finds herself and the grotesque behaviour of people around her – in particular the men. It is a theme which is treated with anger and disgust in *Lo stupro* (The Rape), tragically in her version of *Medea* and comically in *Coppia aperta* (Open Couple) in which the hypocrisies of 'sexual liberation' are dissected.

Dario Fo and Franca Rame have a world-wide reputation. The Scandinavian countries were among the first to welcome them as performers and to produce their work. The whole of Western Europe has by now acknowledged their importance and virtuosity. Ironically the Berliner Ensemble, the theatre founded by Brecht to whom Fo owes so much, found Fo's rock version of *The Beggar's Opera* too difficult to take in spite of Brecht's advice to treat famous authors with disrespect if you have the least consideration for the ideas they express. It had to be staged in Italy. Foreign travel has not been without its problems: attacks on the theatre where they played in Buenos Aires under military rule and a visa to the United States long refused. The summer of 1986 saw the American administration at last relent, which may be some sort of comment on how they judge the Fo's impact and importance in the present political climate.

* * * * *

Archangels Don't Play Pinball was the piece with which the Fo-Rame company opened at the Odeon in Milan in 1959: their début into the big time, as it were. As such it is a daring choice. Technically it is a quick-moving farce which draws on some of the classic situations of the French tradition of Labiche and Feydeau, with bedroom confusions and pompous officialdoms. Its use of the transformation of the hero into an animal looks further back to the literature of the Roman Empire – to the story of Apuleius and his golden ass, who suffered the same fate. The intervention of the archangels at the end is an irresistible reminder of the *deus ex machina* of classical theatre and an interesting parallel to the part played by the gods in Brecht's *Good Person of Szechwan*. True to the tradition of farce the plot is fast moving. It was, Fo says, 'acted with the rhythm of a film, where the scenes, the jokes follow each other with the rhythm typical of a film sequence', in a kind of montage: the technique he had learned in his brief and unsatisfactory career in the cinema. The piece is also unusual in that the cast of twelve – eight men and four women – all, with the exception of the hero Lofty and his girl friend Blondie, play several parts. This doubling of roles originated with the exigencies of the travelling companies; here it is used as a source of farcical complication for the hero keeps recognising the players in their new guises. The social provenance of the characters is also unusual. The young men in what one might call their 'real life' sequences – for the bulk of the play is a dream – are youths from the sub-proletariat who recall the wide boys Pasolini describes in his novels set in the working-class suburbs of Rome. Their butt is Lofty, a simple young man who describes himself as 'the Rigoletto of the poor' – as, in fact, a *giullare*, the innocent who by his literal reading of situations reveals them in all their absurdity. Thus, in trying to claim a disability pension, he finds that he is registered as a dog and to circumvent the intricacies of Italian bureaucracy must submit to being put in a kennel. But the political content is limited to the exposure of civil service absurdities or the pomposity of a ministerial visit to a provincial town – a study of a venal politician on the make. The point was not lost on the Italian audiences of the fifties.

Fo wrote the play in twenty days shut up in a hotel bedroom. He emerged – in the tradition of strolling companies like the one headed by Franca Rame's parents – with a loose sketch to be shaped during rehearsals, which Fo has always demanded should last six or seven weeks during which the gags, the business and the text are polished and tested. Even then there is no guarantee that the text will not be altered; for to Fo a play is something that is subject to development, to adaptation to changing circumstances. What follows is as definitive a text as one may hope to find – at least in English.

STUART HOOD
December 1986

This translation of Archangels Don't Play Pinball *was first staged at the Bristol Old Vic on 10 September 1986. The cast was as follows:*

LOFTY (*Lovely, Cloudy, Stormy*)   Roger Rees

BLONDIE (*Angela*)   Tina Jones

PASTRY COOK   Christopher Ettridge
THE PRIEST
GENTLEMAN AT RECORDS OFFICE
POLICE INSPECTOR
THE MINISTER

ANTONIO   Keith Woodhams
THE DOCTOR
CLERK
THE TRAIN GUARD
DOG POUND KEEPER

BERTO   Tim Stern
CLERK
POLICE SERGEANT
DOG CATCHER
STATIONMASTER
OFFICIAL AT THE OPENING CEREMONY

GIULIO   Roger Ashton-Griffiths
CLERK
DOG CATCHER
CARABINIERE

PIETRO   Neil Boorman
CLERK
DIRECTOR OF THE DOG POUND
THE MAYOR

MARIO   Simon Slater
CLERK
THE CONJUROR
CARABINIERE

ROSA   Rosy Sanders
WAITRESS
WOMAN AT THE RECORDS OFFICE
WOMAN AT THE DOG POUND
COUNCIL OFFICIAL'S WIFE

NATALINA   Helena Mitchell
WAITRESS
WAITRESS AT THE RECORDS OFFICE
COUNCIL OFFICIAL'S WIFE

Directed by Glen Walford
Designed by Claire Lyth
Music by Simon Slater

ACT ONE

Scene One: A street in Milan
Scene Two: A cake shop
Scene Three: A street café
Scene Four: A house in the red light district

ACT TWO

Scene One: A ministry in Rome
Scene Two: A municipal dog pound
Scene Three: At the conjuror's house
Scene Four: In a railway carriage
Scene Five: At the opening of a school

ACT THREE

Scene One: A bedroom
Scene Two: The street café again
Scene Three: A house in the red light district.

Act One
Scene One

Scene: A Street in Milan

The curtain opens on a completely bare stage, with a plain backdrop. Enter seven YOUNG MEN, *dressed identically in white shirts, black trousers and braces. They march in step, to the front of the stage, and begin to sing.*

Chorus:

The night is like a giant umbrella full of holes.
Someone's shot it full of drops of lime.
Like a giant pinball game constructed for King-Kong,
The moon is like a flashing 'Replay' sign.
And my city's like a giant pinball too.
The girls are flipper buttons there to press.
Easy does it, or they'll go into a tilt.
Steady there 'cos this game needs finesse.

Watch out for the tilt! Watch out for the tilt!
A red light isn't my way, gimme a flashing green light 'Replay'.
Watch out for the tilt! Watch out for the tilt!
It's the basic rule of every game, but few can keep it in the brain.
Watch out for the tilt! Watch out for the tilt

We're the toughest, we're the quickest, we're the greatest, we're the gang.
We scare the rich by nicking their dogs and cats.
And when we've terrorised them, so they start to moan and whine
We blackmail cash from these aristocrats.

At night you'll find us prowling in the shadows in car parks.
Stealing radios from the cars.
Easy does it, or they'll go into a tilt.
A shaky hand won't get us very far.

Watch out for the tilt! Watch out for the tilt!
Always block before you shoot – one false move you'll lose
the loot.
Don't set off the tilt! Don't set off the tilt!
If you want to steal, don't be a fool – take my advice and
play it cool.
Don't set off the tilt! Don't set off the tilt!

During this song, the seven YOUNG MEN *are standing
front-stage, in front of a traverse curtain running across the
stage. At the end of the song, one of the* YOUNG MEN *(the tall
one) suddenly topples over, quite rigid. Two of the* YOUNG
MEN *pick him up by the shoulders; two others take him by the
feet. The other two exit stage right.*

LOFTY: Hopla!

FIRST YOUNG MAN: God, you're heavy!

SECOND YOUNG MAN: Hey, don't overdo it with the corpse
bit! You're only supposed to look ill, you know.

LOFTY: How am I supposed to look, then?

THIRD YOUNG MAN: Sort of stiff.

LOFTY: Stiff like this?

He arches his back.

FOURTH YOUNG MAN: What's happened? Have you had a
stroke? Get that belly down!

He tries to flatten his belly with a rabbit punch.

LOFTY: (*Straightening his body with a jerk*) Ouch! Don't *do*
that! (*He ends up on the ground*) Hey, no, that's enough!
I'm not playing any more. You can be the impending
corpse, if you like. I already told you, I never fancied the
part in the first place…

FIRST YOUNG MAN: Ah, so you didn't fancy it? Do you hear that? He never fancied it... And here we are, risking prison. There's gratitude for you!

THIRD YOUNG MAN: What, you don't mean you were actually expecting thanks from monkey-face here, do you? You *must* be stupid!

SECOND YOUNG MAN: We're all stupid! There we go, we get him a wife: a nice bit of stuff, with pots of money, guaranteed a virgin...

FOURTH YOUNG MAN: (*As if reading the banns for a forthcoming marriage*) With her own house and a Very Proper Person... And now, when we try to organise him a decent wedding dowry into the bargain, he has the nerve to say that he doesn't fancy playing the prospective corpse! How ungrateful can you get!

THIRD YOUNG MAN: Don't you think you're pretty damn disgusting?!

LOFTY: (*Tearfully*) Yes, yes, I do... You know, I think I must be a terrible person... really! You're all so good to me... You're always helping me, and I... If you just dumped me here, all alone, it would serve me right. You'd be quite right to spit in my eye... Schplock!

He turns to one of the YOUNG MEN *and spits in his eye.*

FIRST YOUNG MAN: (*Leaping backwards*) Hey, go easy on the self-mortification... I'm already short-sighted as it is...!

He wipes his eye.

The traverse curtain is drawn aside to reveal the inside of a pastry shop.

Scene Two

Scene: A Cake Shop

SECOND YOUNG MAN: Now, I hope you're not going to start whingeing again! Come on, get a move on. Up on my back.

LOFTY: Alright, alright, I'm coming.

He goes round behind the YOUNG MAN *and flings both arms around his neck.*

SECOND YOUNG MAN: I thought I told you to get up on my back.

LOFTY: Well I am on your back. It's not my fault if you've got little legs…

SECOND YOUNG MAN: Will you knock it off, stupid!

LOFTY: Oh alright then, I'll knock it off.

He starts hitting his friend's head. The SECOND YOUNG MAN *humps* LOFTY *up onto his back, and two others take his feet. They go in through the shop door. The* PASTRY-COOK *owner of the shop comes out to serve them. He is alarmed by what he sees.*

PASTRY-COOK: What's the matter with him?

THIRD YOUNG MAN: Would you mind clearing a bit of space on your counter, please.

PASTRY-COOK: Was it an accident? Has he been run over?

SECOND YOUNG MAN: I wish it was an accident… !The odd broken leg, a quick slap-dash with the plaster, and he'd be right as rain. But hunfortunately…

PASTRY-COOK: Hunfortunately what… ?

They lay LOFTY *out on the counter. He groans.*

THIRD YOUNG MAN: Unfortunately, unfortunately! Can't you see… he's dying?

LOFTY *gives what sounds like a dying croak.*

PASTRY-COOK: And you have to bring him into *my* shop to die in the middle of my cakes and pastries!

SECOND YOUNG MAN: You don't expect us to leave him to die out in the street, do you?! Have you no conscience?!

PASTRY-COOK: Alright, then, you'd better call a doctor!

LOFTY *groans.*

THIRD YOUNG MAN: Good idea. Where's the phone?

PASTRY-COOK: (*Passing the phone*) Here you are... Wait, I'll get the phone book... Maybe we'd best call the hospital straight off and ask them to send an ambulance...

FIRST YOUNG MAN: Give it here. If I'm not mistaken, the number's on page 1...

PASTRY-COOK: (*Pointing to* LOFTY) But what's the matter with him?

LOFTY *groans.*

FOURTH YOUNG MAN: Must be a stroke.

Enter one of the YOUNG MEN, *clearing the way for another, who is carrying a doctor's bag.*

THIRD YOUNG MAN: Here he is, Doctor. Over here... Out of the way, lads. Good thing I thought of going to get a doctor. Clear a space!

DOCTOR: Pass me a chair, please.

FIRST YOUNG MAN: (*Each of the* YOUNG MEN *turns his head and passes the order down the line*) Chair!

SECOND YOUNG MAN: Chair!

THIRD YOUNG MAN: Chair!

FIFTH YOUNG MAN: Chair!

PASTRY-COOK: Chair!

In a frenzy of activity, they pass six chairs from one person to another, with the result that, by the time they've finished, all the chairs are back where they started, and still nobody is sitting.

DOCTOR: (*To* LOFTY) How do you feel?

LOFTY: (*Questioning the* DOCTOR *in turn*) How do I feel?

DOCTOR: How should I know?! (*Whispering*) It's you who's supposed to tell me!

LOFTY: I'm supposed to say how I feel? But you told me only to say: Ouch, Ouch, Ouch...

DOCTOR: (*Delivering a swift rap of the knuckles to the forehead*) Shut up!

LOFTY: Shut up. Ouch, Ouch, Ouch.

PASTRY-COOK: (*The* PASTRY-COOK *advances from behind his counter, pushing past* LOFTY*'s friends*) What's the matter with him, Doctor?

DOCTOR: (*Feeling* LOFTY*'s pulse*) It amazes me that this man's still alive! I can't even feel his pulse. (*He makes* LOFTY *sit down*) May I?

LOFTY: Yes, yes, go ahead.

DOCTOR: (*Putting his ear to* LOFTY*'s back*) Breathe in. (LOFTY *breathes in deeply*) Deeper! (LOFTY *does as he is told*) Cough. (LOFTY *coughs*) Harder! (*When the fake* DOCTOR *puts his ear to* LOFTY*'s back, the* FIRST YOUNG MAN *puts his ear to the* DOCTOR*'s back, and so on down the line, with each of the* YOUNG MEN *listening to the next one's back, and ending up with the* PASTRY-COOK *last in line. Each cough makes the listeners jump, with the jump getting larger as it goes down the line, as if the sound signal is being amplified as it goes from one to the other*) Show me your tongue. (LOFTY *does as he says. The* DOCTOR *pulls back one of his eyelids*) Oh dear! (*He shakes his head*) Show me your stomach. (*He feels* LOFTY*'s stomach.* LOFTY *wriggles and squeals, because he is ticklish*) That just confirms what I thought. This man is suffering from third-degree poisoning.

PASTRY-COOK: Poisoning? I don't think so, lads! Unlucky in love, more like.

THIRD YOUNG MAN: What do you mean, unlucky in love! He was supposed to be getting married tomorrow morning.

PASTRY-COOK: Precisely, that's what I mean!

LOFTY: (LOFTY *is listening to his own heart through a stethoscope which he has taken from the* DOCTOR*'s bag*) It's going meep, meep! (*Pointing to the stethoscope*) The line seems to be engaged. We'll have to wait a while.

Madam, would you please get a move on . . . .

DOCTOR: (*Snatching the stethoscope*) He must have eaten something a bit... dodgy. Do you have any idea what it might have been?

SECOND YOUNG MAN: Well, we've all been out for a meal together... But he didn't touch a thing. He was a bag of nerves. After all, this is his last night of freedom!

DOCTOR: (*Searchingly*) Are you sure that he didn't eat a thing?

FOURTH YOUNG MAN: (*With calculated vagueness*) Nothing... No, really, nothing. All he ate was five or six cream puffs he must have bought somewhere or other...

PASTRY-COOK: (*As if the truth has suddenly dawned*) What do you mean, somewhere or other? Come to think of it, I *thought* I recognised that face. He bought his cream puffs *here*!.

FIRST YOUNG MAN: (*Sardonic and menacing*) Ah, so he bought them here, did he? Splendid!

SECOND YOUNG MAN: Oh yes... wonderful! (*They all crowd round the* PASTRY-COOK, *menacingly*) So *you* are the murderer!

PASTRY-COOK: (*Backing off behind his counter*) Hey, I say, don't mess around, lads! You don't really think that it was my cream puffs... They're fresh baked every day... Ten years I've been in this game, and I've never had anything like... And anyway... since you've eaten them too, that just goes to show... !

FOURTH YOUNG MAN: It goes to show nothing of the sort, because none of *us* actually ate any. Luckily, we didn't have time... !

CHORUS: We had a narrow escape!

DOCTOR: (*Authoritarian*) Would you mind leaving your arguments till later. We're going to have to call an ambulance straight away. We'll leave the police to deal with this gentleman.

FIRST YOUNG MAN: Here's the number. (*He dials it, and then brazenly puts his finger down on the phone rest*) Hello…

PASTRY-COOK (*Pleading*) Look, Doctor, there must be some mistake here; it can't have been my pastries…

DOCTOR: (*Curt and dismissive*) That's as may be. Anyway, that's something which can only be decided by the police forensic department.

LOFTY: (*Falsetto*) Oooooh! Ooooouch!

FIRST YOUNG MAN: (*Still holding the phone*) Damn! Nobody's answering! It's always the same when you need them! Never bloody get hold of them! What a bunch of… !

One of the YOUNG MEN *hits* LOFTY, *to make him groan.*

LOFTY: Ouch, Ouch, Ouch!

SECOND YOUNG MAN: (*In heart-rending tones*) Doctor, can't you do something? I don't know, an injection, or something… I can't bear to listen to him!

LOFTY: Ouch, Ouch, Oooooh! (*To his friend*) You see, I can do it all by myself! Ouch, Ouch, Oooooh!

DOCTOR: (*In a professional tone*) I'm afraid that not even a stomach-pump will cure him.

FOURTH YOUNG MAN: (*Sounding like an avid supporter of euthanasia*) Well, if there really is nothing more to be done… maybe we'd better get it over and done with. Let's give him some more of these cream puffs (*He picks up a tray of pastries*), or maybe this cornetto… that way, he'll die quicker.

DOCTOR: This is no laughing matter. Put that filthy stuff away!

They throw the cream horn from one to another, as if it's a ball.

PASTRY-COOK: (*His honour is offended*) I say, Doctor, no… Go easy! Filthy stuff, indeed! That's going a bit far! You'll see… when the public health department has examined my goods…

FOURTH YOUNG MAN: (*Aggressive, stopping him in his tracks*) …They'll shut your shop for good, they'll withdraw your licence, and, more than likely, they'll put you away for life, my dear Dracula!

PASTRY-COOK: (*In a tight corner, but still fighting*) Go easy with the insults! And beware of making insinuations, because…

FIRST YOUNG MAN: (*Not giving an inch*) Because? Because what? Ha! Insinuations he calls them! Everybody knows that your little sweety-puffs are made of… synthetic powders.

PASTRY-COOK: (*Backed onto the defensive*) Well, so what? And who doesn't use them nowadays? Even the big firms use them.

DOCTOR: (*Like a referee stopping a boxing match because one of the contenders is hopelessly outclassed*) Anyway, powders or not, your shop will be closed pending the outcome of the… inquest… which is going to take… *a good, long while*… Anyway, we'd better call the police straight away.

LOFTY: (*Free-associating, as if hallucinating*) Yes, yes, the police! (*He picks up the phone*) Hello. Police… Calling all cars…

He makes a noise imitating a police siren.

DOCTOR: (*Snatching the phone*) That's what we should have done straight away…

FIRST YOUNG MAN: Police? (*He thumbs through the phone directory at incredible speed*) Ah yes, here we are. Police.

He goes over to dial the number.

LOFTY: (*As above*) Yes, yes, the police… and my mummy…

PASTRY-COOK: (*In desperation*) No, please, stop! You can't… If they shut down my shop for all that time, I'll be ruined. Please, show a little understanding! I swear, it wasn't my fault. Don't drive me to ruin.

LOFTY: (*Whining pitifully*) Yes, yes, drive him to ruin! Ouch! Ooooh! I want my mummy!

DOCTOR: (*Humane and understanding*) But look... Even if we take him to hospital, the minute the doctors diagnose food poisoning, they're bound to put in a police report themselves...

FOURTH YOUNG MAN: (*Wickedly*) And after that, you won't even get a permit to sell peanuts!

PASTRY-COOK: (*Tearful, destroyed*) God, what a disaster! What am I supposed to do now? (*The* FOURTH YOUNG MAN *takes his hand, and tries to console him*) I've put everything I had into this shop, and just as business was starting to pick up...

FIRST YOUNG MAN: Ah, at last! I've got the Casualty Ward, Doctor. Do you want to talk with them?

He hands him the phone.

FOURTH YOUNG MAN: Just a minute, listen. (*He pulls out a handkerchief, and as he talks, he mops the sweat from the poor* PASTRY-COOK's *brow. He dries his tears, and even blows his nose. Then, he applies this much-used handkerchief to mopping the* PASTRY-COOK's *face*) I have no way of knowing whether this gentleman is an honest person or not. But just supposing that he is, we can't allow him to be kicked out in the street just by a stroke of bad luck. After all, it's not him who makes the artificial powders – it's the big companies! And, as usual, they're the ones who get off scot-free. It's the same old story – big fish and little fish.

THIRD YOUNG MAN: Let's not start on politics now. Get to the point. What are you saying? You're surely not suggesting that we take our friend and dump him in a ditch, just to save this fellow... ?

LOFTY: Oh, no, not in a ditch... I want my mummy...

SECOND YOUNG MAN: Behave yourself, you, otherwise I'll give you another cream puff.

PASTRY-COOK: (*Snatching the phone from the fake* DOCTOR*'s hand*) Oh, please, can't you do something to help?! After all, sometimes, all it takes is a little good will…

FOURTH YOUNG MAN: (*He picks up the phone, distractedly, and puts it to his ear*) Listen, Doctor, wouldn't it be possible to go to one of those private clinics? Who knows… maybe… with a little application of cash… maybe they'd keep quiet… ?

DOCTOR: (*While taking the phone and pretending to be speaking with somebody at the other end of the line*) Yes, that's a good idea! But do you know how much it would take to hush up a case like this? You're talking about a hundred thousand lire before they'll even look at you!

PASTRY-COOK: (*Taking the phone in turn*) Well, I could certainly put in something. Let's see how much cash I've got in the till…

He puts the phone down and goes to look in his till.

FIRST YOUNG MAN: (*Winking broadly*) No, no, lads, I don't like this business. Compassionate considerations are all very well, but we can hardly be expected to run the risk of winding up in prison, just for his sake. And anyway, supposing this young man dies – someone's going to have him on their conscience!

THIRD YOUNG MAN: (*Turning to* LOFTY) Oi, stupid, groan!

LOFTY: Yes, yes, I'm groaning… Oooouch, Oooooh… Oooouch, Oooooh…

FIRST YOUNG MAN: Can't you see that he's dying?

FOURTH YOUNG MAN: Come on, come on, don't be so stingy! Have you no pity on the poor lad… ? (*So saying, he grabs the wad of money that the* PASTRY-COOK *is holding*) Give it here. How much is there?

He starts counting.

PASTRY-COOK: About a hundred thousand. But if you prefer, I could do you a cheque.

THIRD YOUNG MAN: No cheques, no… The clinic where we're taking him doesn't accept cheques.

DOCTOR: (*Catching the wad of money*) This will do for the moment. Then we'll see…

SECOND YOUNG MAN: Shall I call a taxi?

DOCTOR: No, there's no need. I've got my car parked round the corner. Let's go.

LOFTY: (*Getting up, and making as if to get down from the counter*) Let's go, lads.

He receives a wallop, which flattens him again.

FOURTH YOUNG MAN: Behave yourself, idiot! (*Turning to the others*) Give me a hand.

LOFTY *remains rigid. They hoist him onto their shoulders.*

PASTRY-COOK: (*Going to the door with them*) I really don't know how to thank you, lads… Let's hope that everything turns out for the best…

DOCTOR: Don't worry. The director of the clinic is a very good friend of mine. Actually, maybe you'd better give me a few more of those cream puffs, so that he can analyse them. Once he's discovered the cause, it will be easier to prescribe the cure.

PASTRY-COOK: Please, please, take them all. I'd have had to dump them anyway…

THIRD YOUNG MAN: We'll see to that. (*They grab handfuls of cream puffs and assorted pastries*) Let's take these too. You never know.

One of the YOUNG MEN *grabs a few cakes.*

PASTRY-COOK: Why the cakes? Where do the cakes come into it?

FOURTH YOUNG MAN: Oh they do, they do! Cakes always have a lot to do with it!

They load all the pastries onto LOFTY's *stomach, thereby turning him into a stetcher.*

SECOND YOUNG MAN: You have no idea how much stuff these experts need to make an analysis. See you next time!

PASTRY-COOK: Let's hope not! (*He slumps onto a chair*) God, what an afternoon! (*Distractedly, he picks up a cream puff and takes a bite*) I got off lucky there! I'll never use artificial powders again as long as I live! Mind you, to taste them you'd never think that they were poisonous. Poisonous?! (*He suddenly realises that he has swallowed half a cream puff*) Oh, God, what have I done?! Oh, God, I'm dying. Doctor, wait for me… (*He sticks his head out of the shop*) Hey, you, wait for me! I'm coming too. (*Exit, running*) Oh, God, what have I done!

The traverse curtain is pulled across again, to conceal the shop. The YOUNG MEN *enter, front-stage. They are obviously pleased with themselves, laughing and slapping each other on the back.*

FIRST YOUNG MAN: Ha, ha! It went like a dream! I've never seen such a donkey in all my life!

DOCTOR: I must say, you were all very good. Even I would have fallen for it.

LOFTY: Was I very good too?

PASTRY-COOK: Hey! Stop! Wait for me… !

FOURTH YOUNG MAN: Let's go, boys – Cream Puff's had second thoughts!

They give LOFTY *another wallop, to knock him flat. They load him up again, and off they go. Enter the* PASTRY-COOK.

PASTRY-COOK: They've gone! Where are you… ? Wait for me, I don't want to die!

He runs off after them, but takes the wrong exit.

LOFTY: (*Peering round the wings*) Hey, Cookie, we've gone this way.

He vanishes, and the PASTRY-COOK· *runs back after him.*
Re-enter the YOUNG MEN.

FIRST YOUNG MAN: Talk about a run for your money!

LOFTY: Shame it's over. I enjoyed that!

THIRD YOUNG MAN: We've shaken him off this time.

FOURTH YOUNG MAN: Yes, but don't let's hang about here.
Let's go to the bar. We can relax there.

Scene Three

Scene: A Street Café

The YOUNG MEN *stroll across the stage. Meanwhile,*
stage-left, a small table is brought on, with a number of chairs.
A GENTLEMAN *sits down on one of the chairs, slightly in the*
shade. As the group gets close to him, a spotlight picks out the
GENTLEMAN'*s face. He looks for all the world like the*
PASTRY-COOK.

FIRST YOUNG MAN: There he is again!

LOFTY: Let's go, lads!

He lets himself go rigid again, and topples over. This time
there is nobody to catch him, so he crashes to the ground,
and lies there, motionless. The others all bump into each
other in the general confusion. Some of them trip and fall.

GENTLEMAN: Easy, boys! What's the matter with you?
Antonio, Berto... Why all the hurry?

DOCTOR: (*Suddenly stopping*) Michele, is that you? Good
God, in that light I would have sworn that you were the
pastry-cook. In fact, if it wasn't for his apron, you'd be a
dead ringer...

GENTLEMAN: What pastry-cook?

The YOUNG MEN *re-enter, one by one.*

FIRST YOUNG MAN: Hello, Michele. You gave us quite a fright, there!

THIRD AND FOURTH YOUNG MEN: Who's he, then?

DOCTOR: I'm sorry: allow me to introduce my friends. Pietro, Marco, Luciano… (*as the* FOURTH YOUNG MAN *arrives*) and Giulio.

ALL THE YOUNG MEN: (*Shaking hands*) Delighted… Pleased to meet you…

GENTLEMAN: (*Noticing the trays of pastries*) Are you going to a party?

THIRD YOUNG MAN: We're coming from a party, more like…

DOCTOR: We have just succeeded in diddling a pastry-cook, who is the spitting image of you.

As they are talking, two of the YOUNG MEN *go up to* LOFTY, *who has not moved from the moment he fell over.*

GENTLEMAN: Ah, now I see why all the hurry…

SECOND YOUNG MAN: (*Prodding* LOFTY *with his foot*) Hey, Lofty, wake up, danger's over!

FOURTH YOUNG MAN: Don't worry. Joke's over now. He's not the pastry-cook. (*He pats his face*) Oh good God! He must have knocked himself out… Antonio, come over here… You're good at being a doctor! Take a look…

The DOCTOR *comes over, feels his pulse, and listens to his heart.*

FOURTH YOUNG MAN: (*Aside*) You'd almost take him for the real thing.

DOCTOR: It's nothing. Splash a little water in his face, and he'll be OK… Waiter! A jug of water, please.

THIRD YOUNG MAN: No point in waiting for that waiter to shift himself! I'll go.

He exits.

GENTLEMAN: Let's hope he's not concussed.

SECOND YOUNG MAN: Don't worry. If a person's going to get concussion, it means he's got to have a brain in the first place. I bet his skull's as solid as a billiard ball.

DOCTOR: We only take him along because he's good for a few laughs. We play the daftest tricks on him, and he always falls for them…

He goes to sit down on the only available chair. They whip it out from under him, and he thuds to the floor.

FOURTH YOUNG MAN: Once, we actually persuaded him that he had turned invisible.

One after another, the YOUNG MEN *whip the chair out from beneath each other – and rhythmically, as if in a ballet – they crash to the floor with a loud thud. The last in line, thinking that he has the chair all to himself, goes to sit down. However, the nearest* YOUNG MAN *kicks it out of the way. Final mighty thud. All this action takes place as the* FOURTH YOUNG MAN *continues uninterrupted with his story.*

FOURTH YOUNG MAN: He fell for it too! He went up behind this girl who was walking down the street, and started feeling her up. The best part about it was that she went along with it, but her boyfriend, who was walking next to her, didn't quite see things the same way! Oh, our poor invisible man! He ended up with two big black eyes, and the poor devil couldn't see for two days!

FIRST YOUNG MAN: But the best joke is the one that we're working on at the moment. We're getting him married off to a lady of easy virtue.

GENTLEMAN: To a what?

FOURTH YOUNG MAN: To a tart… A pro-sti-tute.

SECOND YOUNG MAN: Well, actually, she's not a real prostitute, in the sense that she doesn't really earn her living at it, like the others… She's more what you'd call a part-timer.

FOURTH YOUNG MAN: Yes, more like door-to-door service.

Home help sort of touch. (*Imitating a woman's voice*) Can I do you now, sir?

GENTLEMAN: But you're not really marrying him off for real, are you?

DOCTOR: Don't be silly! If we did, where would the fun be? Hang on, and I'll tell you how it's gone so far. (*Turning to the* YOUNG MAN *who has arrived with a jug of water*) Don't wake him up yet. I want to tell the story... And then we'll ask him to give us a hand too... (*Pointing to the* GENTLEMAN) So, for a start, we filled his head with all sorts of ideas... telling him that it was time he got himself a wife, that he couldn't go on living like a tramp for the rest of his life, that he had to do this, that and the other. Then we got him to put a small-ad in the local paper...

FOURTH YOUNG MAN: Hang on, I bet he's still got it in his pocket... (*The* FIRST YOUNG MAN *hunts through* LOFTY's *jacket, until he finds a newspaper cutting*) Here it is; read it out!

FIRST YOUNG MAN: (*Reading*) 'Young man, unemployed, no property, average looks, slight physical defect... '

FOURTH YOUNG MAN: We persuaded him that it's always best to tell the truth.

FIRST YOUNG MAN: (*As above*) '...seeks to marry young lady, rich, extremely beautiful, preferably blonde, must be a virgin, home-owner, and no physical defects.'

GENTLEMAN: Don't tell me he actually went and handed it in at the office! Can you imagine their faces!

DOCTOR: But you should have seen *his* face when he got a letter in reply. Needless to say, we'd sent it ourselves, making out that it was from a rich and very beautiful Albanian woman!

GENTLEMAN: Albanian? Why Albanian?

FOURTH YOUNG MAN: Because Albanians are orthodox Christians, and we've managed to persuade him that, in the orthodox religion, the groom is not allowed to see the bride's face until after the wedding.

THIRD YOUNG MAN: I tell you, this wedding is going to be hysterical! We've found the bride. And, thanks to the pastry-cook, we've also got the money to pay her and her girlfriends…

SECOND YOUNG MAN: (*Pointing to their loot*) Not to mention a wedding cake and pastries galore.

FOURTH YOUNG MAN: And we've even got the priest's coat (*From under his jacket, he pulls out a long black tunic*) Coptic, into the bargain. Now all we need is a priest…

DOCTOR: And I say that we've found the very man… Here he is!

He points to his friend.

GENTLEMAN: Me? Are you crazy?! I could never go through with it. Once I start laughing, there's no stopping me!

FOURTH YOUNG MAN: You can do what you like, it won't matter. He's never going to notice.

SECOND YOUNG MAN: Ssssh, he's coming to.

LOFTY: (*He starts moving his arms, and gingerly feeling the back of his head*) Ooooh! Ooooouch! What hit me?!

FIRST YOUNG MAN: Quick, Father, get into your clothes!

From under his jacket he pulls an Orthodox priest's hat, and jams it on the GENTLEMAN's head. Another YOUNG MAN slips the black tunic around him. They hoist him up onto a table. Then they set a chair on the table and set him down, as if on a throne.

FOURTH YOUNG MAN: (*Patting LOFTY's face*) Come on, wake up. Nothing to worry about. You've just had a little nap!

LOFTY: Eh, who's that… ? Oh, it's you. (*Then he sees the GENTLEMAN*) The pastry-cook! Let's go!

He makes as if to run off.

DOCTOR: (*Sitting him down again*) No, calm down. It's not the pastry-cook. I know it looks like him, but it's not.

FOURTH YOUNG MAN: This is a Coptic priest. We've arranged him specially for your wedding.

LOFTY: A Copt especially for me? (*He gets up, all stiff and aching, and goes over to the fake* PRIEST) Pleased to meet you.

The THIRD YOUNG MAN *signals to him to go down on his knees.*

FIRST YOUNG MAN: Kiss his hand, ignoramus!

LOFTY: (*Kneeling down*) Yes, yes, thank you.

He kisses the PRIEST'*s hand.*

GENTLEMAN: Most welcome, most welcome. Get up, my son.

He turns his face the other way, so as not to let LOFTY *see that he's laughing.*

FIRST YOUNG MAN: You heard what he said. Get up, and pick him up in your arms.

LOFTY: In my arms? Why in my arms?

DOCTOR: Because that's the way that the Orthodox do things. In our country, the groom carries the bride over the threshold. But in Albania the groom carries the bride's priest. Go on, get a move on! In fact, get him up on your back, because it'll be easier.

LOFTY: The bride's priest? On my back? And where am I supposed to take him?

He humps the PRIEST *up onto his shoulders.*

FOURTH YOUNG MAN: Obviously, to the bride's house, idiot! Come on, we'll show you the way.

In the intervening period, a red table cloth has been spread over the table. The table is then lifted up and held over the PRIEST'*s head as a canopy.*

LOFTY: Oh, good, good, so at last I'm going to see her.

FOURTH YOUNG MAN: Now, let's go! Sing!

They move off in procession, singing.

The night is a like a giant umbrella full of holes.
Someone's shot it full of drops of lime...

Blackout. As they exit, the traverse curtain opens again.

Scene Four

Scene: A house in the red light district

We are in the YOUNG LADIES' *house. It is decked with coloured paper festoons. The fake* PRIEST *is binding* LOFTY's *wrists to the wrists of his bride. The* BRIDE *is all dressed in white, and wears a veil which hides her face.* LOFTY *is blindfolded. All the* YOUNG MEN, *together with three of the* YOUNG LADIES, *hold decorated candles in their hands, and sing in chorus:*

Chorus:
Clasp my wrists tightly in your hands
And even with my eyes closed, into your eyes I see.
Clasp my wrists closely to your hands,
And even with my eyes closed, your heart has no mystery.

Please take my love – please take my love
Please take my love – please take my love
I give it freely just for one smile
Please take my love – please take my love
Please take my love – please take my love
I give it freely just to hold you awhile.

PRIEST: (*Stepping between the two of them*) Now you repeat to yourselves, after me: Whatever you look like, whatever your virtues, whatever your faults, I promise to keep you always with me, until death us do part.

CHORUS: Until death us do part!

PRIEST: Always with me, since it is fate that has given you to me.

CHORUS: Until death us do part!

PRIEST: From now on, my shadow will be yours, I shall see light only through your eyes, I shall speak words only through your lips.

CHORUS: Until death us do part!

PRIEST: My blood will pass through your heart, and yours through mine, because we shall be one single being, until death us do part!

CHORUS: Until death us do part!

PRIEST: I now pronounce you man and wife... You may now look at each other.

Two of the YOUNG MEN *busy themselves taking the blindfolds off the couple and untying them. First* LOFTY *has his blindfold removed, and then his* BRIDE. *She is a tall blonde with an open, honest face. Everybody applauds. Then there is silence. The* BRIDE *smiles, and the* GROOM *stands stockstill, as if struck with amazement.*

LOFTY: Oh, I say... !

DOCTOR: Is that all you can say? What do you think of her?

LOFTY: Oh, I say!

BRIDE: Pleased to meet you!

LOFTY: Pleased to meet you! Oh, I say... !

THIRD YOUNG MAN: You could at least say something! She is your wife, after all!

LOFTY: Is she really my wife?

CHORUS: Of course she is, you've just married her.

LOFTY: Oh, I say! Pleased to meet you.

BLONDIE: (*Simply*) Pleased to meet you.

PRIEST: And you, Miss... I'm sorry, Madam... I almost forgot, I just married you... As I was saying, what do you think of your husband?

BLONDIE: Well, he's lovely and tall... Oh, I say, how *tall* he is!

LOFTY AND BLONDIE: (*In chorus*) Oh, I say! Pleased to meet you!

DOCTOR: Well, now we've got you spliced good and proper, long live the bride and groom!

ALL: (*In chorus*) Long live the bride and groom!

THIRD YOUNG MAN: Come on, come on. You're the groom. Make yourself useful. Pour us a drink!

LOFTY: (*Picking up a bottle, while the girls go round with trays of glasses of various sizes*) Listen, Giulio, this won't turn out to be a trick, will it… ?

GIULIO: A trick? What do you mean, a trick? You don't think we're the kind of people who play practical jokes?

LOFTY: No, but you don't suppose she's going to have second thoughts, do you?

GIULIO: Don't worry, she won't have second thoughts… She's never thought a thought in her life, so how can she have second thoughts?

LOFTY: Never had a thought? But she *is* beautiful! Oh, I say… Hey… (*All the* YOUNG MEN *crowd round to kiss the bride and her girl friends*) Me too! Me too! I've got to kiss the bride too! She is my bride, after all… (*For all that he tries,* LOFTY *doesn't manage to kiss her. The* YOUNG MEN *pass her from one to the other, as if in a game of Piggy-in-the-Middle. They laugh uproariously. The* GIRLS *also play along with the game, and let themselves be cuddled by the* YOUNG MEN. *In a whirl of shouting, laughter and movement, gradually everybody disappears off-stage, via various exits. In the confusion,* LOFTY *is left holding the Orthodox* PRIEST *in his arms*) She's my bride… !

PRIEST: What *are* you doing? I'm the priest.

LOFTY: The priest? Oh! (*He takes his hand and kisses it*) I'm sorry, but actually I was hoping to kiss the bride. Where's my bride, so's I can kiss her?

PRIEST: She must be in one of the bedrooms, with one of your friends.

LOFTY: Ah, well, if she's… (*He realises what the* PRIEST *has said, and is thunderstruck*) In one of the bedrooms?! What do you mean?! In bed?

PRIEST: Yes, that's the custom. Your custom over here is that you kiss the bride. But in our Orthodox religion, one goes to bed with the bride. That's our custom…

From stage-right, we hear loud shouting.

BLONDIE: You pig! Take that off, take it off at once!

VOICES: What's got into you…? Hey… Get your hands off!

BLONDIE: Look, that's not your stuff, so you've no right to wreck it!

DOCTOR: (*Entering, wearing* BLONDIE's *wedding dress, pursued by* BLONDIE *in her petticoat*) Alright, I'll take it off! For chrissake, what a spoilsport!

BLONDIE: And go easy, because you'll tear it.

Enter another of the YOUNG MEN, *wearing one of the* YOUNG LADIES' *dresses; then another, and another, all dressed in women's clothing.*

FIRST TRANSVESTITE: (*As the other 'girls' giggle stupidly*) Calm down, girls, calm down. This is a serious matter. Come on, what's all this racket?

SECOND TRANSVESTITE: (*Turning to* LOFTY) Oh, what a big boy! And how good looking! What a shame you're already married, otherwise… just think of the fun we could have had!

THIRD TRANSVESTITE: (*Pointing to the friend with whom he is arm-in-arm*) Excuse me, Mr Priest, we want to get married.

FOURTH TRANSVESTITE: Oh, yes, I've decided to make an honest woman of her… Up till now, you know, we've been living in sin…!

BLONDIE: And now I'm annoyed – get out!

DOCTOR: Hey, Blondie, we had an agreement…

BLONDIE: The agreement wasn't for you to kick up a fuss.

GIRL: Well, what's the matter... They haven't done anything wrong...

OTHER GIRL: God, what a misery-guts you are! Just for one stupid old nightdress...

BLONDIE: But that's the nightdress I go to bed with.

DOCTOR: The nightdress and who else?

Everybody laughs.

BLONDIE: (*Turning to the other* GIRLS) And you can get out too... Go on, scram!

GIRLS: (*All speaking together*) Alright. We're going. Just ignore her... She's just neurotic... ! Goodbye! Come to my house... There you can put on all the women's clothes that you want...

FOURTH TRANSVESTITE: (*As if quoting a proverb*) The only parties you remember are the ones that end badly... See you, love.

FIRST TRANSVESTITE: And to think that this little prank cost us a hundred thousand... I'm still not sure who's the bigger mug here, him or us!

BLONDIE: (*Turning to the* PRIEST, *who is still chanting*) Hey, you, Priest, you can scram, too!

PRIEST: (*Moving towards the exit*) My blessings upon you, my daughter! (BLONDIE *blows a raspberry. The* PRIEST *passes comment on her refined manners*) Charming!

He exits.

BLONDIE: Drop dead, you... ! (*She closes the door*) Oh, at last, they've gone away. I've just about had them up to here!!

She moves across the room.

LOFTY: (*He is still sitting there, at the back of the stage*) What a bunch of jokers, eh?

BLONDIE: (*Not noticing his presence*) You can say that again!

LOFTY: (*Understandingly*) I tell you, once they start, it always seems to end up like this... It's enough to drive a person nuts...

BLONDIE: (*Suddenly realising that he's there*) Hey, what are you doing here? I thought you went off with the others.

LOFTY: (*Insouciant*) Why would I have done that? After all, we're only just married, and it would hardly be right for me to go off, on our first night together... it really wouldn't be right...

BLONDIE: (*She runs over to the window, sticks out her head, and shouts down*) Hey, haven't you forgotten something?

VOICES FROM OUTSIDE: Oh, yes... Lofty! Well, the good Lord gave him to you, so you'd better make the most of him... Ha, ha, ha... ! (*Laughter*) Goodnight, lovebirds!

BLONDIE: You rats... ! And now what am I going to do with you?

LOFTY: (*With not a trace of irony*) Tell me about yourself; about when you were young.

BLONDIE: Eh?!

LOFTY: (*As above, sincere and insouciant*) Well, if we're going to get to know each other, maybe it would be best to start from when we were kids. For example, I remember that when I was a young lad, I was so developed that, at the age of 15, people took me for 10.

BLONDIE: Well, I remember that when I was a young girl, I was so developed, that at 15 they took me for 5.

LOFTY: How's that? Only five?

BLONDIE: Yes, five... five thousand lire... cash.

LOFTY: Ha, ha! (*He laughs happily, and then changes tone*) There's no point in pretending to be a hard-nut with me. It won't wash. I noticed how you trembled when I was holding your wrists... (*He comes up to her and takes up the position of the wedding rite*) Go on, admit it – you were getting all emotional too.

BLONDIE: Well, yes, a little bit emotional, I'll admit… (*She begins taking down the paper decorations, and* LOFTY *gives her a hand*) What with all that chanting, and all those long words. It was pretty powerful stuff! And then the white dress into the bargain… Even an elephant would get all weepy if you dressed it up in a white wedding dress! So there you are: I wasn't getting emotional over you… you or anyone else. It was because of the whole set-up…

LOFTY: Not me or anyone else? But what about when you said: 'Wow, aren't you tall… !'

BLONDIE: Alright, I said that you're tall. So what? You're not going to tell me that you're not tall, are you?

LOFTY: Yes, but when you said that I was tall, well, you weren't just saying it because I'm tall… I tell you, nobody's ever told me that I was tall like that before… Go on, say it again!

BLONDIE: What, that you're tall?

LOFTY: Yes, I like the way you say it.

BLONDIE: Hey, are you making fun of me? Don't take the piss… !

She hurls a bunch of paper decorations in his direction. LOFTY *catches them nonchalantly.*

LOFTY: Me, make fun of you? I wouldn't dream of it – you're so beautiful! And so tall as well… ! Just for you, I'd like to be even taller. Reeeally tall… So that then you'll say: 'Wow, you're reeeally tall'!

BLONDIE: (*Not sure whether to be flattered or irritated*) Listen, pack it in, will you! When you start talking like that, it's like being in a loony bin… ! They warned me that you were a bit weird, but I never realised that you were barmy! (*She approaches* LOFTY, *a touch maternal*) But hasn't it even occurred to you yet, that that bunch of bums…

LOFTY: (*Not reacting to what she says. Preoccupied*) Tell me something, that custom about the groom's friends sleeping

with the bride... I suppose it does only apply to the
wedding night... ?

BLONDIE: What are you talking about? What custom?

LOFTY: (*As if thinking aloud*) No, it really would be too
much. There you are, tucked up with your wife, and one of
your friends comes in and says: 'Excuse me, mind if I
borrow your wife for a while... ' (*She looks at him in
amazement*) If you don't mind, I think we ought to lay our
cards on the table... I'm really not too keen on that kind of
thing.

BLONDIE: What on earth have they been telling you? (*With
angry gestures she begins picking up glasses from around
the room*) Why did I ever get involved in this farce?
Because, damn it, there's no way to have fun with someone
like you! How can anybody enjoy beating someone over
the head, when they just smile at you and say thank you and
you spit at them and they just look at you with a face like
that?!

LOFTY: (*Totally unruffled. Still with his melancholy smile*)
What do you mean? What's wrong with my face? Don't you
like it?

BLONDIE: No, I never said that! It's a bit silly, I suppose, but
at least it's honest...

LOFTY: Yours is honest too.

BLONDIE: (*She looks at him for a moment. She is about to
smile, but suddenly frowns*) Now look, are you going to
leave... ? Can't I ever get a bit of peace... ?

LOFTY: (*He gets up slowly, speaking deliberately*) Alright,
alright, I'm going... Calm down, though! After all, you
haven't done so badly out of this little prank. In fact, they
paid you pretty handsomely. (*Suddenly turning a bit nasty*)
And now you're getting all guilty because you're disgusted
with yourself for having earned your money at the expense
of a poor idiot who just stands here looking at you like
you're Snow White with her seven dwarfs... And so you
start shouting and yelling... Calm down, eh! (BLONDIE

looks at him in amazement) Alright? Calmed down? Right. Goodbye.

He makes as if about to leave.

BLONDIE: Hey, wait a minute…! You're not going to tell me that your brain has started working all of a sudden? What was that little outburst all about?

LOFTY: (*He takes a few steps back into the room. He leans on the back of the chair, and carries on gazing at her with the same melancholic, slightly distant smile*) Oh, don't you worry! My brain has been working all along. I'm perfectly well aware that they make fun of me… In fact, most times it's me who sets up the situation in the first place… That little gang are completely devoid of imagination, and if I didn't give them a hand… they'd be completely incapable.

BLONDIE: (*She drops into a chair, astonished*) Now I *know* you're barmy! Not only do you know that they're making fun of you, but you even give them a hand. Can you explain to me what pleasure you get out of it all?

LOFTY: (*Pulling a cigarette out of his pocket*) It's not exactly pleasure. You see, letting people make a fool of me is more or less my profession.

BLONDIE: A profession?! People making a fool of you, a profession?

LOFTY: Yes. Do you know what jesters were?

He lights the cigarette.

BLONDIE: Of course! (*Erudite and encyclopaedic*) Jesters were people hired by kings and royalty to keep them amused… Correct?

LOFTY: (*Laughing*) Absolutely correct. And that's exactly what I do. The only difference being that since there's no more kings and royalty, I make my pals at the café laugh. In short, I'm the poor man's Rigoletto… But the most important thing is that it provides me with a source of income.

BLONDIE: (*Amazed, incredulous*) They pay you for it?

LOFTY: I tell you, I earn more than if I was a clerk, and I have to work a lot less. Look: every single thing that I'm wearing comes from them; I sleep in their houses, a different house every night; they pay for my meals, my cigarettes, my drink… And if I ask for a little loan now and then, they always oblige… You never refuse an idiot a loan…

BLONDIE: (*She spits on the floor in disgust*) What kind of a man are you! Doesn't it disgust you, the idea of earning your living like that?

LOFTY: (*Adopting the same tone. Provocative*) And what does it do for you, to earn your living in the way that you do?

BLONDIE: (*After a moment's embarassed silence*) Touché! That hurt!

LOFTY: (*Sorry, since he had expected a quite different reaction*) I'm sorry, I didn't mean to say that.

BLONDIE: (*Melancholic, sighing*) No, I deserved it. Here's me, preaching about self-respect! What a joke! It makes me angry. Look – for a woman, when all she's got is her looks, like me, the only way to make money – wrap it up any way you like – is always the same. But for a man…

LOFTY: (*He gets up and, bringing his chair over to* BLONDIE, *sits down next to her*) It's just the same: it all depends on how you start out… It's not that someone like you decides from one day to the next to walk the streets. Either you're born to it, or you work it out as you go along. I'm born to it. My father was the start of it all. Just for a joke, seeing that our surname was Weather, he decided to give me three names when I was baptised: Lovely, Cloudy and Stormy! 'That way you'll be able to pick your name according to what the weather looks like,' he used to say.

BLONDIE: (*First she is amused, but then appalled*) He must have been mad!

LOFTY: (*Warming to his theme*) Mad! I'll say! You ought to try it, with your schoolmates out in the playground… *and* with grown-ups: 'How are you doing? What's the weather like today? Har, har!' Year in, year out!

BLONDIE: (*Not smiling*) It must really get on your nerves.

LOFTY: (*Leisurely, like a story-teller telling of something that's happened to someone else*) Even during the war they tried to make a fool of me…When a fellow gets wounded, he can be wounded in a hundred different places… in an arm, maybe, or a leg… or in the head… But with me, I copped a wound in the parson's nose! A single bullet took it clean away! Wham!

BLONDIE: (*She can't help laughing*) Ha! Ha! (*She gets an attack of hiccups*) Hic… ! But how on earth did they manage to hit you precisely there?! Hic!

LOFTY: Precisely – how on earth! You see? Even you start laughing… and now you're getting hiccups. Even fate thought it was a good laugh to get me hit precisely there.

BLONDIE: Ha! Ha!

LOFTY: Now I'm registered as a Grade 2 War Invalid. I'm supposed to be entitled to all sorts of benefits and privileges, and even a pension. One day I was sitting on a tram, and a fellow asked me to give up my seat to him. He said he was a war invalid. So I answered: 'I'm a war invalid too.' He looked at me, obviously not believing me, and said: 'Where are you wounded?' 'The Parson's Nose,' say I. I'd hardly finished speaking, when he grabbed me by the tie and started shouting: 'Listen, I've got nothing against homosexuals, but I see red when they go round boasting about the fact… ' I tell you, he was within an ace of throwing me off the tram. (BLONDIE *laughs*) And then you're surprised that a fellow ends up playing the fool a bit!

BLONDIE: (*Affectionately*) If you ask me, you bring these problems on yourself. You seem to be always walking around looking over your shoulder, to find out what people are saying behind your back. And then, bang! you crash into the first lamp-post you come to! Hic… ! (*She hiccups*)

And then you start cursing fate for putting lamp-posts on pavements.

LOFTY: Well done! You've summed me up to a T... But sorry to go back to it: if you are so good at rumbling other people's cock-ups, mine in particular, then how come you got caught up in the life you lead?

BLONDIE: (*She picks up a tray and a towel, and continues speaking in a dispassionate tone*) Because when I began, I was more ignorant than I am now. And ignorance really is the worst of all possible evils. My father always used to say... Hic...

(*She repeats this phrase, like a record-player needle stuck in a groove*) My father always used to say... Hic... (*She repeats this phrase, while at the same time cleaning her tray, her hand going round and round as if it were the arm of a record-player resting on a record.* LOFTY *lifts her arm a fraction, and shifts it slightly across the tray, like somebody stopping a record skipping. This done,* BLONDIE *continues talking normally*)

My father always used to say that when a man or woman suffers from the disease of ignorance, they end up like long skinny trees with no leaves. Poles. But even as a pole, I've turned out wonky...

LOFTY: (*Without looking at her; with a tender smile*) Well, I tell you what, you might even be better off being wonky, if you happened to end up with a pole who was wonky in the opposite direction to you... if you tied the two of them firmly at the top... (*Catching his breath*) they would stand a lot firmer than if they were straight.

BLONDIE: (*She steps back to take a better look at him*) Would that happen to be a double meaning... ? (*Hiccuping*) I mean, are you talking about you and me?

LOFTY: (*He slowly gets up, and speaks in fits and starts*) Listen, why don't we pretend that I don't know who you are, and you don't know who I am? Come on... Do you think that you could stay with me?

BLONDIE: (*Almost tripping over herself, and then slowing down*) Stay with you? In what sense… ? Just for tonight? Or for a long time? No, because if it was just for tonight, I would tell you who I am, and I'd ask for the going rate…

LOFTY: (*He drops into the chair. He rubs his hands*) Ah, so now we're getting serious!

BLONDIE: (*Intensely*) Why, what were you thinking… ? Haven't you understood yet that if I'm standing here telling you all this, it's because I think I know what you're all about, and because, bloody hell, I never get a chance to explain things as they are, like I'm doing now.

We hear a knocking.

FRIEND: (*From outside*) Are you home?

BLONDIE: Hic… (*She hiccups*) Go away, I'm busy!

FRIEND: (*As above*) Let me in. I've come to bring you back your clothes.

BLONDIE: Oh alright. (*She opens the door*) Come in… Give them here… Oh, look at the state they're in…

FRIEND: (*Noticing* LOFTY) Oh, is he still here? (*Bragging*) Give me a minute and I'll get shot of him. (*He goes over to* LOFTY. *With heavy irony*) Excuse me, Lofty, I have to talk with the lady about some rather delicate matters. Would you mind shifting your carcase?

LOFTY *does not budge.* BLONDIE *angrily throws the bundle of clothes down onto a chair.*

BLONDIE: He's not shifting anywhere! If anyone's going to shift their carcase, it's *you*. And that means now… !

FRIEND: (BLONDIE *advances on him, menacingly, and he tries to fend her off*) No, you've got me wrong… Look, I'm not just here to fool about… I'm paying like a lord, and, what's more, cash in advance… Look at this… A right little bunch of roses… (*He waves around a bundle of 10,000 lire notes*) Come on, get shot of Lofty. My soul is feeling poetic tonight.

BLONDIE: (*She looks at* LOFTY *for a moment. He is still sitting, lost in thought. She turns to the* FRIEND) You throw him out... And in the meantime, I'm going to put this stuff away! (*Turning to* LOFTY. *In a whisper*) Come on, let me see if you really *are* interested in this wonky pole.

She exits. The FRIEND *has removed his jacket.*

FRIEND: (*Turning to* LOFTY *and pointing a finger*) Alright, now get this into your head...

He tosses his jacket onto a chair.

LOFTY: (*Getting up, as if just waking up*) Alright. I get the message. I'm going...

FRIEND: (*Surprised*) You're going?

LOFTY: (*Turning and coming back*) Why, don't you want me to go?

FRIEND: No... No...

LOFTY: (*He sits down again*) Alright, then, I'll stay...

FRIEND: No, no...! I meant yes, yes...

LOFTY: (*He gets up again, giving him a deprecating look*) Yes, yes, or no, no? If you ask me, you must be a bit stupid. (*He sits down again*) Anyway, you're going to have to lend me a thousand lire for the cab...

FRIEND: (*Without thinking, he goes to hunt through the pockets of his jacket*) A thousand lire...? Why? Where do you have to get to?

LOFTY: To the central police station... At this time of night, it's the only one open.

FRIEND: (*He spins round, abruptly*) To the central police station...? What for?!

LOFTY: (*He crosses his legs in a matter-of-fact manner*) Oh, just to report a couple of small items. Like blackmailing and swindling a pastry-cook... I tell you what, it's weighing on my conscience... The more I think about it, the more I think that I should go and give myself up... You know, now that I'm married, I've decided to turn over a new leaf...

FRIEND: (*Taken aback, and then becoming increasingly aggressive*) Hang on a minute, have you gone completely round the twist?! You're going to end up putting us all behind bars... You are an unthinking, ungrateful, undeserving swine. That's what you are. And I'm going to smash your face in. And to think, we only did it for your sake.

LOFTY: (*Pretending to be taken aback*) Only for my sake... ? In that case, whose is all that money?

He points to the money.

FRIEND: Huh, what's that got to do with it? That's for our pains. We also have to live, friend!

LOFTY: (*He stretches his legs, with an air of boredom*) Yes indeed, you have to live. Now I come to think of it, it wouldn't be such a good idea if I went and gave myself up... Apart from anything else, I'd end up being locked up myself...

FRIEND: (*With a sigh of relief, he presses his point*) And you'd probably end up getting a longer sentence than the rest of us put together.

LOFTY: (*Casual again. Smiling. His speech is punctuated with abrupt gestures. His head inclines first to one side and then to the other*) No. I wouldn't get a longer sentence than you. I'm an idiot... Everybody knows that I'm an idiot... I could always say that you forced me into it... that I really did believe that I was ill. After all, if you can persuade a fellow that he's invisible, and that he's married to a prostitute... then you can make him believe anything. In fact, now I come to think of it, I reckon you'll probably cop an extra few months for taking advantage of someone who didn't know any better...

FRIEND: (*After a brief pause, he suddenly whips his hands out of his trouser pockets and comes up close to* LOFTY, *with an air of amazement*) Hey, I say... is that you talking, or some brother of yours, with a university degree, that you've been keeping in mothballs. It looks to me as if you were just *pretending* to be stupid, so that you didn't have to pay your rounds... Will you look at this son of a bitch... ! Just imagine... We thought that we were taking you for a ride...

LOFTY: (*With a calculating and provocative smile*) Indeed... Isn't life amazing... Just when you think that one thing is happening... it turns out that something quite different is going on... This money, for example... (*He points to the money which is sticking out of the* FRIEND'*s pocket*) ...there's you, thinking that it's all yours... But in reality (*He snatches the money from him*) ...now it's all mine!

FRIEND: Give me that your money... or I'll smash your face in...

He grabs LOFTY *and pulls him to his feet.*

LOFTY: Another little thing that I forgot to tell you... I've got a pretty good right hook... (*He delivers a swinging righthander. Then, booting him up the backside, he kicks him out of the door*) Get out! Get out!

FRIEND: You're going to pay for this, Lofty! You won't be so bloody cocky when the others get to hear about this...

Re-enter BLONDIE.

BLONDIE: Hic! (*She hiccups*) He's right... The others won't let you off so easily, that's for sure... It'll be bye-bye jester.

LOFTY: Now you mention it, I reckon my first mistake was coming and spilling the beans to you.

BLONDIE: (*She hiccups*) Hic!

LOFTY: Look, if you try drinking from the wrong side of a glass, maybe your hiccups will go.

BLONDIE: What?

LOFTY: Like this. Look. (*He takes a glass full of water. He bends over and drinks from the opposite side of the glass. The water spills all over him. He coughs*) As I was saying, maybe my first mistake was coming and telling you everything. Maybe I'd have done better to keep it to myself.

BLONDIE: (*She also tries the business with the glass. She takes a deep breath afterwards*) Hey, they've gone.

LOFTY: Good, I'm glad... Hic... ! (*He in turn begins to hiccup*) Now I've got them!

BLONDIE: I'm sorry... What were you saying about keeping it to yourself?

LOFTY: I was saying that maybe if I'd kept quiet, I wouldn't have ended up going away emptyhanded, like I'm going to have to do now.

BLONDIE: You're going away? (LOFTY *nods in the affirmative*) And where are you going?

LOFTY: Well, I've got enough money for a bed for the night... (*He shows her the money that he's just snatched from the* FRIEND)... and maybe I've even got enough to get me down to Rome...

He hiccups.

BLONDIE: To Rome?

LOFTY: Yes. I want to see if I can get my hands on all the pension money that's owing to me... Once I get that, it's going to be a lot easier to walk down the street without having to look over my shoulder all the time, as you were saying... Hic... ! (*He hiccups*) Well, goodbye. It's been a pleasure.

He holds out his hand.

BLONDIE: (*Slowly, almost embarrassed, she takes* LOFTY's *hand*) Goodbye. It's been a pleasure.

LOFTY: A pleasure, what?

BLONDIE: What do you mean, a pleasure, what?

LOFTY: (*Teacherly*) When a person says that something's been a pleasure, they're also supposed to say their names. What's your name?

BLONDIE: Angela...

LOFTY: Hic! (*He hiccups*) Angela?

BLONDIE: (*She holds his hand, tenderly*) Yes... really my real name is Angelica... but, you know, with the kind of work that I do... calling myself angelic would sound a bit silly. So, there you go... when my parents baptised me, they could hardly have known that I would end up here, eh?

LOFTY: True enough! And anyway... Angela is nicer... (*He smiles at her. He tilts his head to one side*) Goodbye, Angela. I do hope we meet again.

He hiccups.

BLONDIE: Goodbye... We *will* meet again, eh? Watch out, because it's dark on the stairs.

LOFTY: Don't worry. I can see where I'm going.

BLONDIE: Goodbye. (*We hear a loud crash offstage*) What happened?

LOFTY: (*From offstage, sounding as if he is only barely refraining from a string of curses*) Damnation! You're right. It's true, I really do walk around looking over my shoulder... I didn't see the steps...

BLONDIE: Have you hurt yourself?

LOFTY: (*From offstage*) No, it's nothing.

BLONDIE: Have your hiccups gone?

LOFTY: (*From offstage*) Let's hope so.

BLONDIE: Goodbye.

LOFTY: Goodbye, Angela. We'll meet again.

BLONDIE: Wait, wait!

LOFTY: (*From offstage*) Yes?! (*There is a note of expectation in his voice*)

BLONDIE: I've got something to tell you. Um... What should I call you? I mean, which of your names do you prefer to be called by?

LOFTY: (*After a short pause to indicate disappointment, he speaks up, in a tone of euphoria*) Call me Lovely... because as from this evening, I'm really glad that my father gave me that name.

BLONDIE: Goodbye, Lovely.

LOFTY: Goodbye, Angela.

Prolonged noise of somebody falling downstairs.

BLONDIE: If that doesn't get rid of his hiccups, then nothing will!

(*She laughs. She picks up a transistor radio. She turns it on, and hangs it round the neck of a tailor's dummy which stands in the centre of the room. We hear the faint strains of the song: 'Clasp my wrists tightly'*)

…Lovely …Lofty LovelyWeather…Yes, he's right. It's very tempting to play about with it…

(*She begins to hum along with the tune coming from the transistor radio. She peers through the curtains and looks down into the street below. Slowly she begins to get undressed. She kicks her shoes in the air, one after another*)

…'Clasp my wrists tightly'

(*She picks up the jacket that has been left on a chair. Lost in thought, she goes to slip it on the tailor's dummy standing back-stage. She takes the dummy in her arms. She mimes a passionate embrace. Only then does she notice that this was* LOFTY's *jacket*)… But this is Lovely's jacket… Oh hell! I sent him out in his shirt-sleeves… Oh, I hope he comes back to get it… In fact, he must come back… He can hardly go to Rome without a jacket… He'll have to come back… And when he comes through the door, I'll say: 'Dear Lovely, if you want to take your jacket, you're going to have to take me too'. (*She tries to imitate* LOFTY's *voice*) 'But what do you mean – before, you rejected me… !' 'But now I'm saying yes… I've had second thoughts… I could really hit it off with a good-looking wonky pole like yourself… '

(*Once again, she embraces the dummy*) Come here, come here, let me bind you to me… Come on, don't tremble like that. Whew! How my heart is beating… ! And yours? (*She puts her ear to the dummy's chest. We hear a knocking at the door*) I say, that's going a bit far! (*She realises that somebody is knocking at the door*) Is that you... ? Have you come back to get your jacket... ? Come in.

(*She suddenly realises that she is in a state of half undress*) ...No, wait, don't come in yet. (*She goes and hides behind a screen*) There, now you can come in. (*Enter the* FRIEND *whom we saw a few minutes previously*) ...But don't come round here. I'm sorry if I kept you waiting, but I was already undressed. I know it's silly for me to want to hide... Don't think I'm being a prude – not a bit of it. But, I don't know... when I'm with you, I feel shy... I know it sounds stupid, but that's the way I am... Mind you, I've said and done so many stupid things today...

She slips on a dressing gown.

FRIEND: (*Flattered, strutting like a peacock*) Well...

BLONDIE: No... don't say a word, otherwise I won't be able to tell you something which I absolutely must tell you, because otherwise I'm going to burst... I've discovered that I've got a crush on you... Don't laugh... I've really got a crush on you... (*By now the* FRIEND *is strutting like the king of the castle*) I realised it the moment you went away, because the minute I saw your jacket, I immediately thought to myself: 'I hope he comes back to get it, because then... then I'll make sure that he takes me too!' Oh, there, I've done it... ! (*She laughs*) Aren't you going to say anything... ? I knew that you'd be stuck for words... It took a lot for me to say it too, you know, and now I'm really glad that I have said it... (*She comes out from behind the screen*) Here I am...

BLONDIE *is completely taken aback when she sees the* FRIEND *standing there, his face wreathed in smiles.*

FRIEND: (*He comes over to her, walking like a cock rampant*) Good God, I must be some kind of magician... I've bewitched you! And just think, I thought you didn't even like me... You see how mistaken a person can be... (*He comes round behind her, running his hand up her back*)

Well, let's go… and you'll find that you've not made a bad choice… (BLONDIE *doesn't move*) Hey, I mean, I hope my magic looks haven't turned you to stone… ! Come on, Goodlooking. (*He gives her a little slap*) Wake up. I'll take you to beddy-byes.

BLONDIE: (*She responds by giving him a mighty wallop*) Get out! (*She starts hurling at him everything she can get her hands on*) Get out, get out, get out!

FRIEND: Alright… I'm going, I'm going… But look, there's no need for you… hang on a minute…

He exits, and once again we hear a terrible crash on the stairs. The FRIEND *has taken a tumble.* BLONDIE *bursts into tears and runs over to the dummy. She looks at it for a moment, and then, with a kick, she sends it flying. The transistor radio hanging round the dummy's neck tumbles to the floor.* BLONDIE , *worried, picks it up, switches it on, and shakes it, to make sure that it's not broken. The radio is still working. We hear the voice of a* RADIO ANNOUNCER, *saying:*

VOICE OF THE RADIO ANNOUNCER: …Over the rest of the country, we will have Lovely Weather. That was the weather forecast up until noon tomorrow.

BLONDIE *bursts into tears and hurls the radio to the floor.*

Act Two
Scene One

Scene: A Ministry in Rome

Enter five CLERKS. *They are wearing black trousers, black waistcoats, and clown-style bald wigs, whose bottom edge is adorned by a thick fringe of hair. As a sign of their office, each carries a rubber stamp hanging round his neck. They march on, in front of a partition made up of a series of little windows. Wheeling to the right, they march towards the footlights, singing, and move around the stage with the grotesque gestures of clerks. They open doors and drawers, they type, they stamp documents etc.*

Kings of the Ink Rubber Stamp

To glorify Egyptians they built a pyramid,
A statue for King David, Charlton Heston made El Cid.
In memory of Columbus, America they named.
Nelson for his column he's famed – we spit on them.
Da Vinci has his painting the Mona Lisa
And even though it's leaning, there's the tower of Pisa.
Each with his monument they go down in history.
Cleopatra has her needle, the housemaid her knee.
Tell me

CHORUS:

The name of the man who sat at his desk over averages, figures and norms
Multiplying, dividing, subtracting and adding, checking the census forms.
Let us sing of the deeds of the Lords of the rates and the social security,

Imbursing, permitting, discharging and taxing, and adding
on V.A.T.

Tell me

The name of the man who sat at his desk over records,
insurance and dole,
Writing chronicles, catalogues, calendars, analogues, tying
up every loophole.
We brothers unite, for a statue we fight, for our work at the
office desk lamp.
We stacked up the piles of red tape and files. We're the
Kings of the Ink Rubber Stamp.
We're the Kings of the Ink Rubber Stamp.

VERSE:

St Mark has got his square, Bolshoi his ballet,
An arch for Julius Caesar and his 'Et tu Brute'.
Eiffel has his tower. Granny Smith has her fruit,
Not denying Wellington his boot – we spit on them.
Khyber has his pass in far off India.
And bright up in the sky, the magi had their star.
Each with his monument they go down in history.
Achilles has his heel and Earl Grey his tea.

LINK:

It hurts us in our hearts there's no monument for us.
Who can name a famous bureaucrat? We die anonymous!
Tell me

CHORUS TENDING:

We stacked up the piles of red tape and files,
Multiplying, dividing, subtracting and adding,
Imbursing, permitting, discharging and taxing,
Chronicles, catalogues, calendars, analogues!
We're the Kings of the Ink Rubber Stamp.

The five CLERKS *take up positions in their respective
cubicles. During the song, the shutters of these cubicles were in
raised position. Now they all drop shut, except for the first one,
which remains open. Enter a* WOMAN. *She goes straight to the
first window and briskly begins sorting out some business.*

Enter LOFTY. *He has with him a very heavy suitcase and a parcel. He goes straight over and starts queueing behind the* WOMAN. *When it comes to his turn, the shutter on the cubicle suddenly drops, and almost simultaneously one of the others open.* LOFTY, *encumbered by his parcel and the suitcase, but more particularly puzzled by the fact that the* LADY *bears a strange resemblance to one of* ANGELA's *girlfriends, is slow to reach the other window. As a result, he is pipped to the post by another* GENTLEMAN, *who comes in at that moment.*

LOFTY: Hey, now look, I was here first… That's cheating, diving in like that!

GENTLEMAN: I haven't dived in anywhere…

LOFTY: (*He notices a curious resemblance of the* GENTLEMAN *to one of his friends*) Hey, the Albanian vicar… What are you doing, here in Rome?

GENTLEMAN: I beg your pardon…

LOFTY: Come off it, you can't fool me… Even if you have grown whiskers!

GENTLEMAN: You're the one who should come off it… Particularly when you pick on someone who has neither the time nor the inclination…

LOFTY: I'm sorry, but I mistook you for a friend of mine who hasn't got a moustache… Anyway, seeing that you've got a moustache, you hang onto it… Alright? Friends again? Come on.

At this point another window opens.

GENTLEMAN: Look you, I'd advise you not to go making fun of my moustache… Here you are, the window's all yours… But thank your lucky stars that I'm in a hurry… Because otherwise…

He moves over to another window.

LOFTY: Alright, keep your hair on… So, I passed comment on your moustache… Well look, it's not against the law to be rude about people's moustaches, particularly because, luckily for us, priests don't wear them any more.

All of a sudden, the window at which LOFTY *is standing drops shut. He is momentarily angered, but then has no choice but to go and get in the queue behind the* GENTLEMAN, *who glares at him malevolently. A* LADY *comes in, and joins in the queue behind him. The* LADY *bears a striking resemblance to the second of* ANGELA's *girl friends.* LOFTY *looks at her, and then ventures:*

LOFTY: Excuse me, excuse me. You know what, you're the spitting image of a friend of mine who's a...

LADY: (*She is irritated. She cuts him off in mid-sentence, and glares at him*) I beg your pardon?

LOFTY: ...who's a... I mean... I mistook you for an auntie of mine who's a Red Cross nurse in Torremolinos.

Meantime, another window has opened. The LADY *leaves the queue and goes over to the window, having picked up the suitcase that she has had with her since she entered. The* LADY *moves pretty fast, and while the* GENTLEMAN *is taking his time, the* LADY *prepares to leave the window.* LOFTY *picks up his baggage, and prepares to move into the vacant space. But the* LADY *has second thoughts, turns round, and comes back to the window.*

LADY: Oh, I forgot... Could you write me out a list of the forms that I have to get from the Council? Thank you...

LOFTY *is caught on the hop for a moment, and, as in the game of Piggy-in-the-Middle, is temporarily wrong-footed. In other words, the* MAN *behind him is about to leave;* LOFTY *tries to move in a hurry; but since he's laden down with baggage, he gets there too late. In his haste, he has picked up the suitcase belonging to the* LADY, *who immediately shouts after him.*

LADY: I say, young man! Will you stop fooling about! My suitcase, if you please!

LOFTY: Oh... yes... I'm sorry, my mistake...

LADY: A likely story! First you're 'mistaken' about who I look like, and then you're 'mistaken' about my suitcase.

LOFTY: Please, I hope you don't think… Leaving aside the fact that our suitcases really are pretty similar… You don't seriously think that I'm about to start on a career as a suitcase thief, do you… cardboard suitcases at that! (*Reaching the window*) Listen, if you don't mind… (*With a great thud, the second window, which the Lady has only just left, closes*) It's all your fault! Why the hell didn't I leave you at home!

So saying, he gives a mighty kick to the LADY'*s suitcase.*

LADY: I say, have you gone mad?

LOFTY: Oh, I *am* sorry… I mistook it for mine…

LADY: Again?!! Thank your lucky stars that I'm not a man.

LOFTY: Indeed I do, indeed I do… ! (*He bends down to give a little rub to the spot he kicked. Then he goes over to the window, which, with malevolence aforethought, shuts in his face*) I'm going to demolish this… repeat-action confessional! (*The* LADY *exits, haughtily.* LOFTY *turns round and trips over his own suitcase. He gives it a look of pure hatred. He steps back to give it a kick, and then pauses for a moment, with his leg raised. Enter a* WAITER, *with a tray, cups and a large coffee pot. He too looks like one of the* FRIENDS *from previously*) Giulio… !

WAITER: My name's Sergio, not Giulio… And anyway, if you want something, you're going to have to order it from the bar yourself. I only serve the clerks…

He rattles a teaspoon in a coffee cup. As if by magic, the rattle of the coffee cup causes the shutter on the first window to open. The WAITER *holds out a cup. The* CLERK *behind the window takes the cup, and shuts the window in* LOFTY'*s face as he runs up, holding out a document.*

LOFTY: If you don't mind, I would like…

Meantime, the WAITER *has gone on to the next window. A rattle of cups. The window opens, and* LOFTY *leaps forward.*

LOFTY: Excuse me, if you don't mind… (*The action is*

repeated. LOFTY decides to play it clever. He doesn't bother about the third window, but goes and crouches next to the fourth window, ready to slip in his document the minute the CLERK shows his face. The coffee cup rattles, and the window opens. But it is not the fourth window. It is the fifth window, the one behind LOFTY. LOFTY spins round hurriedly, but he's too late. The CLERK has already taken his coffee and shut his window) What about this one... Doesn't he get coffee?

He points to the window which had remained closed, and goes over to the WAITER.

WAITER: No. He has tea....

He picks up a larger cup from his tray, and slips it through the window which has opened to receive it, and which then promptly shuts again.

LOFTY: Hey, now, that's ENOUGH! I left my friends, to get away from their stupid jokes, and now here's their doubles playing even worse jokes on me!! *(LOFTY gives his suitcase a terrible kicking. He lets out a yell, and begins hopping around in pain. Meantime, the WAITER nimbly retrieves the cups, which the CLERKS pass out to him one after the other, immediately closing their windows afterwards, like some kind of clockwork mechanism. LOFTY contrives to get a finger caught under one of the shutters)* Ouch! My finger... !

WAITER: *(Sniggering provocatively)* Ha, ha! What a splendid squashed finger! I've never seen such a squashed finger... *(The WAITER continues laughing unabated, and does not notice that the GENTLEMAN from previously has entered. He bumps into him. He drops a number of coffee cups on the floor. The windows re-open. The CLERKS laugh in unison, and then close their windows. The WAITER, assisted by the GENTLEMAN, picks up the broken crockery. Then, with his cloth, he tries to clean the GENTLEMAN's jacket, which now has coffee stains on it. They apologise to each other. The WAITER gets so engrossed in this paroxysm of cleaning that he even ends up* *taking the* GENTLEMAN's *hands and polishing his nails in the manner of a manicurist*) I'm sorry, I didn't see you...

GENTLEMAN: Me neither. I was concentrating on my paperwork. I'm afraid I've caused you a bit of a disaster!

WAITER: Oh, it's nothing! What about your jacket, though? Look at the sleeve, it's got stains all down it.

GENTLEMAN: A bit of water should take care of that...

WAITER: Well, let's give it a go... (*He spits on the jacket, and tries to clean it off with his own sleeve*) Like I say, I'm really sorry.

He goes to walk off, but LOFTY *deliberately thrusts his suitcase in front of him. This time the* WAITER *takes a tumble verging on the catastrophic. A mighty crash, and there's broken crockery everywhere. The* GENTLEMAN *rushes over to help the* WAITER *to his feet, but* LOFTY *kicks his parcel in front of him. Another crash. The windows open, and the* CLERKS *stick their heads out in order to get a better view of the disaster. They laugh.* LOFTY *ducks and runs up to the windows. One by one he contrives to shut them, in such a manner as to trap the* CLERKS' *heads underneath, as under as guillotine. Then he gives a mighty kick to the* WAITER, *who has only just finished picking up all his bits and pieces, sending him flying out of the door. The* GENTLEMAN *gets the message, and exits running. The* CLERKS *all shout for help.*

LOFTY: That's enough! Silence... ! I said that's enough! Shut up! Listen to me! (*He locks the door*) And now that finally I have the honour and the pleasure of your attention, you're going to listen to me... I have come here on very important business: my pension. I've brought all my papers with me...

(*He opens his suitcase and pulls out a big packet of documents. He waves a bundle of papers, which he then shoves, one by one, under the noses of the* CLERKS. *One each*)

Birth certificate... Residence permit... Permanent

discharge papers... Long-term invalidity certificate...
Permits on headed paper... Permits on plain paper...
Pre-dated permits... Supernumerary permits... And a
reserve permit just in case. I don't understand what a single
one of these is about... But I have done my duty, and now
you are going to do yours: verification, signature, and
rubber stamps. I want all the marks and countermarks,
rubber stamps, stamps and counterstamps that may be
required... so that when I leave here, I want to go away
with all my papers in order, so as to get my pension.

(*He moves fast, and grabs the rubber stamps which the*
CLERKS *have hanging round their necks. By virtue of the
fact that they are hanging on elastic, he succeeds in
positioning a rubber stamp on the forehead of each of the*
CLERKS. *Then he moves over to one side. He grabs a lever
which is connected to the long partition that runs down as a
counter, under the cubicle windows, onto which he has
already slapped his papers, ready for stamping*)

I've got no time to waste... And just in case there's any
messing about, here I've got a little present that I brought
back from the war, which, I assure you, I shall explode right
under your noses the minute I suspect that anyone here is
trying funny business... Here you are, take a look: a model
38 hand grenade. (*He pulls a hand grenade out of his case,
and sticks it on the doorman's desk*)

Round rubber stamps! (*Two of the* CLERKS *bring their
heads down with a thud, and stamp the papers*) Square
rubber stamps! (*Two other* CLERKS *do the same*) All
rubber stamps together! Stamp, stamp, stamp! Stamp,
stamp, stamp! All rubber stamps together! (*The* CLERKS
do not do as instructed) All stamps together! (*They still do
nothing*) I said: all stamps together! (*They still do nothing*)
Damn – it's jammed! (*He gives the lever a hefty pull, so that
the counter begins to jiggle rhythmically to and fro, under
the noses of the* CLERKS, *whose heads, with the rubber
stamps strapped to their foreheads, bob up and down in
alternating rhythm, stamping his documents. The overall*

impression is of an extraordinary futuristic machine)
Stamp, stamp, stamp, stamp!

(*As the rhythm speeds up, the whole sound effect transforms into the chuffing of a steam engine, rattling along, with a final 'toot-toot' as the whole apparatus comes wheezing to a halt*) Toot-toot… Toot-toot… Ding, ding… We've arrived!
And now all I need is my registry document, which, obviously, we're going to find under the appropriate entry in one of the filing cabinets.

(*Along one side of the office runs a wall completely occupied by filing drawers.* LOFTY *pulls out the drawer that he is looking for*) A's over there, S is over here. So W must be over here. Ah, there it is. (*He sticks the drawer under the nose of the first* CLERK) There you go, find my filecard.
The name is Weather, Christian names Lovely, Cloudy, Stormy, and God help anyone who laughs, because he'll get a punch on the nose!

(*The* CLERK *succeeds in pulling out a card, parrot-style, using his teeth*) Here we go with the lucky draw! Some you win, some you lose! Well done! You've picked the very one!
It's me: Lovely Weather… Born in… Distinguishing marks… Breed: Retriever dog… ! No… ?! Ah, yes…
Breed: Retriever dog. Profession: Hunter of birds. Tail docked, large floppy ears, short canines, appears to be a mongrel… Ha! Ha! (*He laughs, hysterically*) So I appear to be a mongrel?! (*The* CLERKS *laugh.* LOFTY *picks up his hand grenade and pulls out the pin. The* CLERKS *stop laughing*)

Whose bright idea was it to pull a filthy trick like that on me? Come on, spit it out. Who was it? I warned you, don't play the fool with me… Don't try and act clever! These days I don't even let my friends play tricks on me… And they *pay* for the pleasure… ! Sign me up as a retriever, would you?!
(*He raises his arm as if about to throw the hand grenade*)
You're going to pay for this! Go ahead, laugh! Laugh for the last time! Go ahead… Ha, ha, ha! (*The* CLERKS *want to shout for help, but they are struck dumb with terror*) Roll

up, roll up! Coconut shy! Four balls for a shilling! Ha, ha, ha...

We hear banging and knocking at the door.

VOICE: Open up... What's going on!? Open up!

LOFTY: Will you just look at those faces... ! Ha, ha...

Blackout.

During the blackout we hear the sound of the door being forced, and a lot of shouting.

VOICES: Stop him... Look out, he's got a bomb! Get a hold of him!

LOFTY: Take good aim, gentlemen. First prize, a medal. A toy monkey for the gentleman, and a balloon on a string...

The way he laughs sounds for all the world like a madman. The lights come up again. We now find LOFTY *handcuffed to a chair. In front of him sits a* POLICE INSPECTOR, *and next to the* INSPECTOR *stands a* POLICE SERGEANT *in plain clothes.*

LOFTY: (*Eyeing them up from head to toe*) A balloon on a string... (*He appears to recognise them*) Here we go again: another two look-alikes! (*Turning to the* POLICE INSPECTOR) Excuse me, you wouldn't happen to have a twin brother in Milan, who's a pastry-cook half the time, and an Orthodox priest the rest... would you?

INSPECTOR: An Orthodox priest?

LOFTY: (*All in one breath*) Yes, an Orthodox priest... well, he's not a real Orthodox priest... he just dresses up as an Orthodox priest. Anyway, he was the one who married me... not in the sense that I married a priest... I wouldn't dream of it... but the fact is that you have a striking resemblance to the pastry-cook too... in fact, that's just what I said to myself: it's amazing how much that fellow looks like the pastry-cook!

During this speech, LOFTY *moves his arms and handcuffed hands from side to side, in a movement that suggests the unwinding of a skein of wool.*

INSPECTOR: That'll do. I said THAT'LL DO! Listen, there's no point in your carrying on like this. (*Caught up in the game, almost without realising it, the* POLICE INSPECTOR *moves his hands from side to side as if he was rolling the wool into a ball*) Don't think you'll get away with passing yourself off as a lunatic. I've seen it all before. (*He suddenly realises the absurd game he's caught up in; he throws away the imaginary ball of wool. The* SERGEANT *catches it and puts it in his pocket*) Come on, now, there's a good chap: what's your name?

LOFTY: And yours?

INSPECTOR: What do you mean: 'and yours'? Leaving aside the fact *I'm* the one putting the questions round here...

LOFTY: What?! You? Still?! Hey, that's not fair... Come on, let's take turns. Lets ching up for it... Shall we let him play too? Yes, let's. (*He waves his hand up and down as in the children's counting game*) Right. One, two, three... Say when... One, two, three, four...

INSPECTOR: When!

LOFTY: When, on the four... Good. (*He begins the count*) Four, five, six, twelve, thirteen is out and I'm in... It's your turn... (*He points to the* INSPECTOR) He's not playing.

He points to the SERGEANT, *who gives him a sideswipe.* LOFTY *parries the blow with the palm of his hand. Another sideswipe, followed by another parry. The movement becomes almost mechanical. The result is a game very similar to that played by children: Pat-a-Palm. In the end, the* SERGEANT *ends up getting a wallop.*

SERGEANT: Are you going to stop fooling about, or not?! Are you going to answer the Inspector's question?

LOFTY: Ah... so you're an Inspector? You should have said so... I thought it was a bit odd for pastry-cooks and Orthodox priests to start slapping handcuffs on people... Well, Inspector, you know what I say? I quite like you!

SERGEANT: (*Losing patience and giving him a backhander*) Watch it, sonny. Who asked you to get so familiar?

LOFTY: And the same goes for you. Is there some section in Police Regulations which says that a Police Inspector can address a citizen in familiar terms, but a citizen can't do the same back?

SERGEANT: I said watch it, laddy! Who do you think you are?!

He gives him a resounding slap in the face.

LOFTY: Hey, no! No, all this whacky-whacky is getting a bit out of hand… Goodbye.

He makes as if to leave.

INSPECTOR: (*Restraining him*) Calm down, calm down… Come and sit down here… Alright, if you insist, from now on, it'll be surnames only, alright?

LOFTY: No, tell you what, Inspector, I've had second thoughts. Let's use Christian names. It's more intimate. After all, we're getting on so well now…

INSPECTOR: Speaking of getting on, you're beginning to get on my nerves… ! (*He gets himself under control again, after the* SERGEANT *signals to him not to carry on in this vein*) Right, if you don't mind, name and surname!

LOFTY: Lovely, Cloudy, Stormy Weather…

SERGEANT: (*Beside himself*) Stop taking the piss, because even if the Inspector is a patient man, I'm not!

He gives LOFTY *another backhander.*

LOFTY: Hey, that's not fair! Hitting a man when he's down!

Seeing another backhander coming, he ducks.

INSPECTOR: Listen, you! (*The backhander hits the* INSPECTOR)That will do, Sergeant! (*Turning to* LOFTY, *grinding his teeth with rage*) Am I going to have to wait long?

LOFTY: If the Corporal here is going to carry on like this, then I'm not saying another word, and that's that… Anyway, Lovely Cloudy Weather really is my real name. If you don't believe me, look at these papers. In fact, this one in particular… (*He points to a sheet of paper sticking out of his case*)… and then you'll see…

SERGEANT: (*He picks up the document and reads*) REHTAEW YLEVOL…

INSPECTOR: (*Looking at him pityingly*) Sergeant! You are reading it upside down!

SERGEANT: Ah, yes. (*He turns the sheet of paper the right way up*) Lovely Weather, that's exactly what it says here…

He hands over the document.

LOFTY: Cloudy and Stormy are my two other Christian names. I told you so…

INSPECTOR: (*Reading the heading on the sheet of paper*) War Office, Statement of Permanent Invalidity… Ah, so you're a war invalid?

LOFTY: Yes indeed. Grade 2… (*Speaking to the SERGEANT, who has literally gone white as a sheet*) Incidentally, Sergeant, I don't quite remember where I read it, but I believe that there are very serious penalties for people who perpetrate violence on a war invalid… Particularly when the above-mentioned finds himself in a position of being physically unable to defend himself… ! Oh·dear, Sergeant, you'll be in trouble now… !

He gives him a wallop.

INSPECTOR: Let him go, Sergeant!

The SERGEANT *removes the handcuffs.*

LOFTY: Isn't life funny! A person moves heaven and earth to advance his career, and one day, just for a silly little thing, it all vanishes before his eyes! All because of this nasty habit of slapping people about! Naughty, nasty hands… ! (*He slaps the back of the* SERGEANT*'s hands. The* SERGEANT *wants to retaliate, but* LOFTY *stops him*) Tut, tut, Sergeant, don't forget… War Invalid! You can't even touch a war invalid with a flower. Would you like a word of advice? If I were you, I'd put the handcuffs on yourself!

Mechanically, the SERGEANT *goes as if to put the handcuffs on himself. He suddenly stops, realising what he's doing.*

INSPECTOR: Alright. Shall we continue? Sergeant, would you mind taking notes, please? (*The* SERGEANT *pulls out a notebook*) Right. Let's start again. Christian name: Lovely; surname: Weather... Did you get that? (*The* SERGEANT, *much chastened, signals yes, by nodding*) Profession?

LOFTY: Hunting dog. Breed: retriever...

INSPECTOR: (*Not thinking*) Hunting dog... (*He suddenly leaps to his feet*) Now then! This is going *too* far! (*He is beside himself. He comes face to face with* LOFTY) Nobody takes the piss out of me. Not even real criminals! I can see we're going to have to sort you out!

LOFTY: Remember the war wound, Inspector... Think of your family!

INSPECTOR: Alright... (*He sits down again, fuming*) But I warn you, war wound or not, if you don't stop piss-balling about... even if it means me being transferred to Sicily...

LOFTY: For heaven's sake, to Sicily! Don't have yourself sent to Sicily, Inspector. That would upset me terribly!

INSPECTOR: Let's get to the point. (*He pulls the hand grenade out of his pocket*) Where did you get this bomb?

LOFTY: But you don't really think it's a real bomb? Can't you feel from the weight that it's empty? Allow me. (*He takes it from the* INSPECTOR, *half unscrews it, and then, turning to the* SERGEANT, *pretends to throw it*) Sergeant, you're dead!

The SERGEANT *takes a leap backwards, and ends up sitting on the* INSPECTOR's *knee.*

INSPECTOR AND SERGEANT: (*With their hands raised in surrender*) Let's not play jokes.

LOFTY: I'm not joking at all! Right, come on, behave yourselves. Read what it says here... Out loud! (*He hands* *them the Registry document with which we are already familiar*) Go on, read it, in chorus!

He threatens them with the hand grenade.

INSPECTOR AND SERGEANT: (*They speak in unison, the one sitting on the other's knee, and moving their arms and hands simultaneously, in such a way as to appear like Hindu dancers*) Lovely Weather, born 24th March 1924 in Sangiano; Breed: Retriever dog.

LOFTY: With his tail docked, and apparently a mongrel!

INSPECTOR: It's incredible!

LOFTY: Indeed it is incredible! And just think, a moment ago you wanted to smash my face in and run the risk of being transferred to Sicily, just because you thought I was making fun of you… And how do you think *I* feel, when I come here to get my pension, and discover instead that I'm supposed to be paying DogTax, as well as going round with a collar and name-tag round my neck, and a muzzle and lead into the bargain?! And then you complain if a fellow every now and then feels the urge to chuck hand grenades around.

He makes as if to throw the grenade.

INSPECTOR: Alright, alright, let's see if we can get this dirty business sorted out as best we can. But for the moment calm down, and put that contraption away…

LOFTY: Don't worry. There's no danger. It's a cigarette lighter. (*He opens it up, turns the flint wheel, and lights the wick. With the flame,* LOFTY *lights himself a cigarette*) You see. Even this is a joke… I play a joke on you…

He tosses them the curious lighter with its wick still burning. The INSPECTOR *and the* SERGEANT *manage to catch it.*

INSPECTOR AND SERGEANT: No!

They in turn throw the trick lighter back to LOFTY.

LOFTY: (*He catches it*)… And you play a joke on me… and that way the whole world becomes a joke… But don't worry, I'm used to it. I won't get upset!

INSPECTOR: I will, though. I can't stand jokes. (*They begin the performance again, in a series of gestures that build to a frenzy*) Especially when they are played by civil servants and officers of the state, to whom has been entrusted the task of seeing to the rights and well-being of our citizens. (*To* SERGEANT) I understand your devotion to your superiors but I'm going to ask you to get up.

SERGEANT: (*He gets up*) Of course.

INSPECTOR: (*To* SERGEANT) Sergeant, I want you to introduce me to every clerk in this office, one by one... Get a move on! Now I'll show them! They'll find out what happens to people who play silly tricks on honest citizens!

The SERGEANT *opens the door abruptly, and all the* CLERKS, *who had been listening at the keyhole, come tumbling into the room.*

SERGEANT: Ah, listening at the keyhole, were we?!

INSPECTOR: Good, well done, make yourselves at home. That means that I'm not going to have to waste time explaining what I want from you. Let's have you! (*The* CLERKS *line up in front of him*) Right, what's the story behind all this nonsense?!

He walks up and down the line, as if reviewing troops, waving the document under their noses.

LOFTY: (*Walking behind the* INSPECTOR, *obviously well-pleased*) Come on, let's have you!

INSPECTOR: I see, nobody knows! Alright, then, I'll tell you what it is: it's a joke in very poor taste... This is making fun of honest citizens!

LOFTY: (*Prompting him*) ...who pay their taxes!

INSPECTOR: ...who pay their taxes...

LOFTY: ...who pay your wages...

INSPECTOR: ...who pay... Hey... gently!

LOFTY: Yes, yes, gently. But you'll see. We'll get to the bottom of this.

INSPECTOR: I want the person responsible for this deplorable and dishonourable act, which is a disgrace not only to your profession, but to all civil servants...

LOFTY: (*Still prompting*) ...including me.

INSPECTOR: ...including me! ...And it is precisely in defence of the honour and dignity... of...

LOFTY: (*As above*) ...the aforementioned...

INSPECTOR: ...of the aforementioned... thank you... that I demand to know the name of the feckless, anti-social individual whom you are protecting! I give you three minutes to tell me, after which...

LOFTY: I'll bang you all up against the wall!

INSPECTOR: I'll bang you all up against the wall!

LOFTY *goes through the motions of a firing squad with a machine gun. He pretends that his gun jams. He mimes taking it apart, and then puts it back together, transforming it into a violin, on which he plays a brief 'fugue'.*

LOFTY: Well, maybe banging *everyone* up against the wall... would be a bit much. We'll just have a little firing squad: one, two, three...

He begins counting off the CLERKS.

FIRST CLERK: (*Taking a step forward*) May I speak?

LOFTY: No!

INSPECTOR: (*As if in a daze*) No!

SERGEANT: (*Servile*) No!

INSPECTOR: One minute, that's all you've got...

LOFTY: (*Parroting him*) That's all you've got...

FIRST CLERK: I believe that I, on behalf of my colleagues, may be able to offer some small explanation of the matter in hand...

LOFTY: You see, Inspector? A mass execution generally proves pretty effective... Sergeant, take this down!

FIRST CLERK: The origins of the problem before us undoubtedly go back fifteen years.

SECOND CLERK: In other words, to the war.

FIRST CLERK: One of our older colleagues was forced to take early retirement, so that he never made it to the higher grade...

THIRD CLERK: ...to which, by rights, he was due to be promoted within a matter of months...

Each of the CLERKS *takes a couple of steps forward in order to make his point, and then, after finishing his contribution, steps back into line.*

LOFTY: Not a bad joke, that! I'll have to add it to my collection.

FIRST CLERK: I was saying... The clerk on whom destiny had played such a terrible joke...

LOFTY: I didn't know that you called your bosses here 'destiny': Chief Destiny... Inspector Destiny...

INSPECTOR: If you don't mind, let's finish...

LOFTY: So, what did our poor unfortunate friend do?

FIRST CLERK: He almost went mad...

FOURTH CLERK: And, determined to take revenge, he began to make alterations and modifications to the census material in the Registry.

SECOND CLERK: And since he had been in charge of this section for the last 30 years, you can imagine the total chaos he created.

THIRD CLERK: In fact, by the time he'd finished, we had: a bishop married to a lighthouse keeper.

FIRST CLERK: A man who died two years before he was born.

FIFTH CLERK: A general who turned out never to have done his military service.

SECOND CLERK: Another was brought back to life twenty

years after his death, and expatriated to America, where he changed sex and married...

THIRD CLERK: ...a barman from the Bronx. (*As the* CLERKS *step in and out of line, their movements begin to suggest a kind of folk dance, with skips, cross-overs and turns*) However, all these changes and alterations were only carried out on the persons (and the relations) of the colleagues and superiors whom he considered responsible for the insult inflicted on him!

LOFTY: (*Interrupting his exposition*) Alright, fair enough. But why pick on me? What have I ever done to the man, to deserve being turned into a retriever dog, and a mongrel to boot?

FIRST CLERK: Have you by chance any relatives working in the Ministry?

LOFTY: No. I'm from Lombardy.

FIRST CLERK: Somebody with a similar name, perhaps... ?

LOFTY: What do you mean, similar name?! Not everybody has the good fortune to have a father as mad as mine!

SECOND CLERK: He must have just got carried away with changing registry entries...

LOFTY: (*Almost hysterical*) But why did he have to get carried away with me? I'll give him carried away! By the time I'm finished with him, he'll *need* carrying away! (*He grabs one of the* CLERKS *by the scuff of the neck*) Where is he... ? I'll give him pension! Where do I find him?!

SECOND CLERK: In the cemetery!

LOFTY: He's dead?!

THIRD CLERK: Yes. He died two months later. They say he never stopped laughing... and that his laughter was so infectious that all his relations round the death bed got caught up with it... It appears that they even laughed at his funeral...

FIRST CLERK: What do you mean, 'appears'? I was there,

and I tell you, it was the funniest funeral I've ever been to…

ALL THE CLERKS: (*In chorus*) God, what a laugh we had!

LOFTY: Alright, alright, let's forget funny funerals and get back to our story! I would like to know how you've been able to get away with this state of falsified chaos!

The CLERKS *begin moving in different directions.* LOFTY *sits down to watch.*

FIRST CLERK: At the start we were all desperate – particularly our superiors. The alterations had been carried out so carefully and skilfully that in order to put right everything that he'd undone, we would have had to call in every single person concerned…

SECOND CLERK: Not to mention people who were already dead.

THIRD CLERK: And people who were not even born yet…

FIRST CLERK: Inevitably, there would have been a scandal… And an inquiry (*With all these people coming and going across the stage, the* SERGEANT, *standing centre-stage, puts on a pair of white gloves and pretends to be directing traffic*) …Followed by an equally inevitable trial, not to mention the ridicule which would be heaped on everyone involved in this tragic circumstance – most of them rather extremely highly placed.

The INSPECTOR *too is caught up in the game, but he ends up crossing the stage just as the* TRAFFIC COP/SERGEANT *has raised his hand to signal stop. The* SERGEANT *pulls out a whistle and blows on it, repeatedly. He is about to book the* INSPECTOR *for a traffic offence. However, the* INSPECTOR *pulls out his police warrant-card, and waves it under the* SERGEANT's *nose.*

SERGEANT: (*Stopped in his tracks*) Ah… Consider it not said, sir… (*Turning to the others, who have formed a huddle behind him*) Keep moving, keep moving! (*Turning to the* THIRD CLERK) You, drive on.

THIRD CLERK: Well, we were saved by a fortunate mishap –

one wing of the Ministry building was obliterated during an
air raid. So we collected up all the falsified documents and
burned them, and their loss was put down to the air raid...

ALL THE CLERKS: (*In chorus*) A Very Good Idea!

LOFTY: All the documents, except mine!

THIRD CLERK: Precisely, except yours. I can't imagine how
yours slipped through!

LOFTY: (*He slowly gets up, looks them up and down, one by
one, as if reviewing them, and then addresses them
aggressively*) Ah, so you can't imagine, eh? Well, I'll tell you
why... Because yours truly is not one of the Firm. Ergo et
propter hoc, who gives a damn... ! Well, a bomb might have
saved you last time round, but this time it's going to blow
you sky-high! Ha, ha! (*To the* INSPECTOR *and the*
SERGEANT) Except you two of course. I'll use the law to
throw you all out in the street... (*To the* INSPECTOR *and*
SERGEANT) And we'll see about you, after.

Now I begin to understand why your mad colleague
involved me in all this. I was the reserve detonator, in case
the first one failed to go off... Ha, ha! (*He laughs, and turns
and picks out somebody in the audience, as if he has just
discovered the deceased come back to life*) Hey, I don't know
about mad... ! You've been pretty clever! Ha, ha! You
prepared your counter-move in advance... You were right
to go out laughing... ! Ha, ha... ! Listen to him laugh... Ha,
ha!

SERGEANT: (*Seriously worried*) He's off his rocker...

INSPECTOR: Calm down! Don't get overexcited, it's bad for
you. We'll sort it out, you'll see. Sit down and relax. Leave
it to me.

Everybody rushes about getting chairs for LOFTY *and the*
INSPECTOR, *who, inevitably, end up sitting down,
missing the chairs, and going down with a thud.*

LOFTY: Relax, he says!

INSPECTOR: (*Paternalistically*) Now, let's see: if I'm not mistaken, you came here to get your pension speeded up a bit. But it's going to take years before all this is sorted out. Don't forget that you'll only get your true identity back when the trial proceedings are over. So the first thing to do is to sort out your position on the Registry files. (*To the* CLERKS) And since all of you, to a greater or lesser degree, are responsible for this state of affairs, you'd better get cracking...

FIRST CLERK: Well, as regards his Registry Office entry, there *might* be a way... But it all depends whether the gentleman is prepared to collaborate...

INSPECTOR: (*Turning to the* CLERKS) Just a minute. I've been bending over backwards, but I can only go so far. If everything is not sorted out within three days, I am going to put out an arrest warrant for your whole department and you'll all end up with a nice long remand in custody pending trial. Understand? Goodbye!

SERGEANT: (*To the* INSPECTOR, *as he exits*) Farewell, Chief!

INSPECTOR: Farewell, my friend! (*He exits, and then immediately comes back on stage, walking backwards, as if in a film that has been run in reverse*) Understand? Goodbye!

He signals to the SERGEANT.

SERGEANT: Oh, yes...

He falls in behind the INSPECTOR. *They exit in step, with the* SERGEANT *setting the rhythm with his whistle.*

LOFTY: OK, spit it out! What is this idea that you've come up with?

ALL THE CLERKS: Excuse us.

They group themselves in a huddle, as if in a rugby scrum.

FIRST CLERK: (*Coming out of the circle*) If you could be so kind as to continue being a retriever... just for a few more days, then...

LOFTY: (*Shrilly, meanly*) Then what… ?

SECOND CLERK: (*Falteringly*) …then everything would be resolved: three days is all it would take… (*He consults with his colleagues in a whisper. They concur*) Naturally, you're going to have to give us a hand.

LOFTY: (*With irony, not convinced*) Oh yes, naturally. What am I supposed to do?

FIRST CLERK: (*All in one breath*) Have yourself caught by one of the city dog-catchers without a muzzle, or without the regulation name-tag round your neck…

LOFTY: (*Shrilly, almost screaming*) What?

THIRD CLERK: (*Backing off, ready to make a run for it*) Obviously, the dog-catcher would be in on what's going on. The Director of the City Dog Pound is an ex-colleague of ours, and would certainly not refuse us such a teeny-weeny favour.

LOFTY: (*Calmly, chewing it over word by word*) So, to cut a long story short, I'm going to have to pass myself off as a stray dog. And what happens then?

FIRST CLERK: (*Reassured, but not very much*) Well, as you know, by law, after three days in captivity, if nobody comes to claim a stray, then the dog is put down in the gas chamber.

LOFTY: (*Lost in thought*) Yes, I know… strays are… (*With a start. Shrilly, as above*) In the gas chamber?! I'm afraid I'm not too keen on this particular little scheme. I'm going to have to think about it.

FOURTH CLERK: (*With an affable smile*) But what on earth did you think we meant… ? Obviously, we're not suggesting that you go to the gas chamber! (*As if explaining the most obvious thing in the world*) Once the three days required by law are over, then it will go down in the records that you, as a dog, have been put down. When this little difficulty is out of the way, you will be able to come back to us, with any two suitable witnesses, and regain your true identity.

THIRD CLERK: (*In the same tone*) And then, on the same day, you will also be able to draw everything that's owing to you on your pension, which, if I do a quick sum, must amount to something like... (*All the* CLERKS *raise their hands, with their fingers spread out.* LOFTY *is made to do the same. The* ACCOUNTING CLERK *does his sums by flicking their fingers up and down, as if he was pressing the keys of a calculator*) Don't mind me... Eight million lire...

LOFTY: (*Enthusiastically*) Eight million! So that's why they call it the Parson's Nose! It must be holy! If that's the kind of money we're talking about, then... let the dog-catcher come! Better to spend three days as a poor dog than a hundred days as a poor man... ! Long live the bureaucracy!!

All the CLERKS *step forward to the footlights, and, in chorus, sing their bureaucrats' song. The traverse curtain is drawn across behind them, so that the scenery behind it can be changed.*

CLERKS: (*In chorus*)

The name of the man who sat at his desk over averages, figures and norms
Multiplying, dividing, subtracting and adding, checking the census forms.
Let us sing of the deeds of the Lords of the rates and the social security,
Imbursing, permitting, discharging and taxing, and adding on V.A.T.
Tell me
The name of the man who sat at his desk over records, insurance and dole,
Writing chronicles, catalogues, calendars, analogues, tying up every loophole.
We brothers unite, for a statue we fight, for our work at the office desk lamp.
We stacked up the piles of red tape and files. We're the Kings of the Ink Rubber Stamp.
We're the Kings of the Ink Rubber Stamp.

Blackout.

Scene Two

Scene: A Municipal Dog Pound

The lights come up. The traverse curtain opens. We are in the municipal Dog Pound. There are several kennels/cages around the edge of the stage, and one in the centre, on which we see a notice, which reads: 'Beware of the Man'. Enter LOFTY, *dragged in most unwillingly by the* DOG CATCHER. *He is wearing a muzzle, and has a dog collar round his neck. The* DOG POUND KEEPER *opens the central cage, and tries to push him in. One of the* DOG CATCHERS *tries to drag him in by tugging on his lead.*

LOFTY: Hey, go easy with that lead, , you're bloody throttling me... Let's have some manners, for heaven's sake!

FIRST DOG CATCHER: Well, get a move on, then... If all mongrels were like you, I'd be long since dead and gone. Come on, get your things off!

Once again, he tries to shove him into the centre cage.

LOFTY: (*Wrenching himself free, and shouting shrilly*) What do you mean?!

SECOND DOG CATCHER: It's the regulations.

KEEPER AND DOG CATCHERS: (*In unison, as if reading the rules*) The captured animal must be stripped of any accessories that it may be wearing at the moment of capture. To whit: lead, collar, name tag, doggy coat, etcetera.

LOFTY: (*Waving his arms like the conductor of an orchestra bringing a piece to an end*) Alright, alright: I get the message. I see you've learnt your lines. Seven out of ten for effort! (*In a bad mood*) Anyway, as far as accessories goes, all I've got is a collar and muzzle. So, cop this lot, and much good may they do you! (*He takes off his 'accessories' and hurls them at the two* KEEPERS) And you can stop taking the mickey, because I only agreed to take part in this charade so as to do a favour for your friends. So, start behaving a bit sensibly, because otherwise I'll kick up a rare old shindig, and you can kiss your jobs goodbye... They'll send you out catching cats! Alright?

He moves closer to the SECOND DOG CATCHER.

FIRST DOG CATCHER: Alright! Alright! But as you know, the regulations state that...

LOFTY: (*He goes into the cage, but comes out again immediately, holding his nose*) Speaking of regulations, what's the vile smell in this place? Regulation smell, is it? (*In the tone of a Duty Corporal*) Let's have you! Scrubbing brush, soap and hot water, because we're going to see some changes round here... ! Come on, jump to it! Move it, move it... !

The two of them unthinkingly leap to attention. The FIRST DOG CATCHER *turns on his heel and exits*.

VOICE FROM LOUDSPEAKER: Your attention please. In a few minutes we shall be opening the gates to admit visitors to the Municipal Dog Pound. However, we must ask visitors not to tease or annoy our animal guests in their cages, and not to feed them. In particular you are advised not to get too close to cages which display notices saying: This Animal Is Dangerous. You are also reminded that access to the gas chamber, particularly when it is in operation, is restricted to the animals in question.

LOFTY *listens attentively, while the* FIRST KEEPER *returns with a scrubbing brush and a bucket of water, and busies himself cleaning up. Enter several* VISITORS. LOFTY *wanders round the cages and stops in front of one of them. He removes the sign attached to the bars. A* LADY *stops in front of the cage on the right*.

LADY: (*Speaking in an oochy-coochy tone of voice*) Nice doggy, nice doggy... Oh, you're a lovely pointer.

LOFTY: (*Going up and standing behind her*) That's not a pointer, madam, it's a retriever.

LADY: (*Without turning round*) How can you say that with such certainty?

LOFTY: Because I'm a retriever too!

The LADY *turns round with an amused smile. In the meantime,* LOFTY *has put his muzzle on. Seeing him, she lets out a scream, and exits, running.*

FIRST DOG CATCHER: (*Running up*) What's the big idea...? What are you doing, going round frightening the ladies? Do you want me to get a ticking-off from the Director? (*He grabs him by the collar*) Come on, get into your cage. It's clean now!

LOFTY: (*Enjoying himself, and imitating the playful barking of a puppy*) Alright. But now will you please leave me in peace, because I want to read for a while. (*He pulls a newspaper out of his pocket*) Please tell reception that if anyone calls, I'm not in. Would you mind shutting the door? Thank you.

He opens the newspaper in front of his face, while one of the DOG KEEPERS *hangs a sign on the bars of the cage. An odd-looking* GENTLEMAN, *dressed in old-fashioned clothes and wearing a bowler hat, comes up to the cage. He takes a look at the sign, and then gets up on tiptoe in an attempt to see who is hiding behind the newspaper.* LOFTY *barks. He peeks over the top of his newspaper, and then ducks back down. Then, irritated by the stranger's curiosity, he moves aggressively over to the bars, snarling and growling like a mad dog.*

GENTLEMAN: (*He takes a startled leap backwards. For a moment, he is completely taken aback. Then, very politely, he turns to the first* DOG CATCHER, *who is still loitering about with his cleaning gear*) Excuse me, are you quite sure that this is a retriever?

FIRST DOG CATCHER: (*Openly making fun of him*) How should I know? I'm not a dog-spotter – I'm only paid to catch them. But if the sign says he's a retriever, then that's what he is.

GENTLEMAN: (*Convinced. Without even a trace of irony*) Good. Alright. I'll take him.

FIRST DOG CATCHER: (*Convinced that he's making fun of him in return*) What?

GENTLEMAN: (*Serious, and even more determined. He passes over a handful of money*) There's the money for the fee… And here are my particulars. I'd like to take it away with me now.

FIRST DOG CATCHER: So, you want to play silly bleeders, eh?

GENTLEMAN: (*With a madman's logic. With feeling*) I can't imagine what makes you think that. Am I or am I not fully within my rights to take the dog that I choose, as and when I want it? And this is the animal that I want.

LOFTY: (*He has been following this conversation with great interest. Suddenly he reaches one arm out between the bars, and grabs the bowler-hatted* GENTLEMAN *by the collar*) Listen here, you pre-Raphaelite nincompoop (*He is referring to the* GENTLEMAN's *late nineteenth-century dress*) If you dare say one more time that this animal, namely I myself, yours truly, 'interests' you, then you're going to get such a boot in the duodenum that you'll end up needing emergency surgery for suspected acute appendicitis! Alright?

GENTLEMAN: (*Dumbfounded. Turning to the* DOG KEEPER) Excuse me, was that him talking, or are you a ventriloquist?

SECOND DOG CATCHER: (*Freshly arrived on-stage*) Allow me to explain, sir… (*Aside, to the other two*) Leave this to me. I know this one. He's nuts. (*With a big wink, he puts his arm around the* GENTLEMAN *and steers him away from the cage, speaking sympathetically, in subdued tones*) You see, it's a bit of a sad story. I'll admit that this fellow appears to be a dog… But the truth is, he's a man…

GENTLEMAN: (*He takes a sideways look at* LOFTY, *to see if what the* DOG CATCHER *said is true*) Really? That's amazing!

SECOND DOG CATCHER: (*Sighing. With feeling*) Yes. He's a man. Poor devil. He's gone out of his mind.

GENTLEMAN: (*Terribly upset*) Out of his mind? Why?

SECOND DOG CATCHER: (*As above*) It's a sad story. He used to have a dog, but the dog ran away, was caught by us, and was put into that cage. By the time he arrived to collect it, the poor devil was already dead.

GENTLEMAN: (*With a lump in his throat*) In the gas chamber?

SECOND DOG CATCHER: (*After a brief pause*) No, suicide… Maybe he thought his owner had abandoned him… (*Sighing*) And, in a moment of depression…

He makes a gesture with his hand, to indicate cutting his throat.

GENTLEMAN: Suicide?! And how did he do it?

SECOND DOG CATCHER: (*He gestures to indicate somebody shooting themselves, but then has second thoughts, and decides on something else*) He slashed his wrists with a piece of broken glass. You see, the owner's wife had also died by the same method, and, as you may know, dogs are very quick to learn.

GENTLEMAN: (*He gazes into the middle distance, as if lost in thought*) You don't have to tell me. I had a dog once, which was an alcoholic. (*He nods his head in the direction of* LOFTY's *cage*) Poor man. So, he went mad with grief? But what's he doing in there now?

SECOND DOG CATCHER: (*He takes him under his arm again. Together, the two of them stroll down the footlights*) Every day, at visiting time, he comes here and asks us to let him go into the cage where his faithful friend passed away. We can't find it in us to refuse him, poor devil – it's heartbreaking!

GENTLEMAN: (*He stops, still half lost in thought*) Ah yes, I know what you mean… I certainly know what you mean. I found it terribly painful when Garibaldi died.

SECOND DOG CATCHER: You were a Garibaldi supporter?

GENTLEMAN: (*Proudly*) No. I was a conjuror! A Republican, but a conjuror! And Garibaldi was a mustard-coloured poodle puppy. (*Delightedly he traces the dog's shape in the air*) And when he'd been to the poodle parlour, with that pom-pom on his head, and those big blonde ears flopping down around his chin, he looked just like Garibaldi as a young man. (*He pauses briefly, giving the* DOG KEEPER *a fixed look*) You know, he was really intelligent. He had even learned how to do conjuring tricks. (*His voice takes on a tone of splendour*) Can you imagine it, a conjuring dog. Splendid, he was!

SECOND DOG CATCHER: (*Giving him full rein*) Good heavens! A conjuring dog?

GENTLEMAN: (*As if about to crack up*) Yes. But the problem was that he died on me just a couple of days before his debut. (*He sighs, and adds, very sadly:*) When he died, I felt as if I was about to go mad.

The SECOND DOG CATCHER *sniggers to himself.*

GENTLEMAN: (*Suspiciously*) What?

SECOND DOG CATCHER: (*Embarrassed. Trying to make amends*) I said: I can well believe it.

GENTLEMAN: (*Toying with the label on* LOFTY*'s cage. Suddenly he turns on the* KEEPER, *very annoyed*) And to think that I almost fell for it… Might one know why you have been spinning me this pack of lies?

SECOND DOG CATCHER: (*Taken aback*) What pack of lies?

GENTLEMAN: Don't try and be clever! The description on this label matches exactly. Retriever dog: docked tail; big ears; unmarked coat; thick dark hair on the head; and short canines. There's no doubt, it's him!

LOFTY: (*Turning aggressive, he thumps the* GENTLEMAN

on his bowler hat. Then he puts his arm round his neck and pulls him back against the bars) Spot on! Yes, I am the afore-mentioned retriever! And since I am also an evil-minded, idle mongrel, if you don't shove off at once, I shall have your ear off. (*He loosens his grip*) And I warn you that I've got rabies, distemper and scabies all rolled into one... So if you're not careful, as well as losing an ear, you're likely to snuff it too.

GENTLEMAN: (*Terrified. Straightening out his dented bowler hat*) Is it true what he says?

FIRST DOG CATCHER: (*Barely restraining himself from laughing in his face*) Completely true. Can't you see what a rabid face he's got?

GENTLEMAN: (*Hysterical*) But have you no sense of responsibility? Why haven't you put a 'Danger' notice on his cage, in case he bites someone?

He backs off, as Lofty romps around his cage, howling.

LOFTY: Uhuuu! Uhuuu! Grrrr! Uhuuu!

The mad CONJUROR *has barely left the stage, when another* GENTLEMAN *arrives. Running up, he grabs the bull-whip from one of the* KEEPERS, *and begins lashing out at* LOFTY.

DIRECTOR: Good dog... ! Down! Down!

LOFTY: Ouch! Aaargh! Uhuuu! Uhuuu! (*The whip catches him on one leg. He hops about, whining*)

DIRECTOR: Down, boy! (LOFTY *sits down at once. With an authoritarian air, the* DIRECTOR *turns to the* DOG KEEPERS) And what do you think you're playing at ? Aren't you capable of keeping this animal under control? What kind of dog keepers are you?

FIRST DOG CATCHER: (*Trying to grab the whip from his hands*) Hey, what is this? April Fool's Day? Who are you?

DIRECTOR: I am the Director.

He takes a step forwards, and contrives to jam his foot into the cleaning bucket.

SECOND DOG CATCHER: Who are you kidding! If you don't mind, I know our Director. He's Dr Campironi.

DIRECTOR: He *was* Dr Campironi. But as from this morning, he's been transferred to another post. (*He frees his foot from the bucket*) …and seeing that as from this moment *I* am Director, you'll do me the honour of making a few changes round here, because otherwise you'll get a taste of my whip too.

He takes another step forward, and sticks his foot in another bucket. While trying to get his foot out, he props himself up next to the central cage.

LOFTY: (*Quick as a flash, he grabs the whip. He wraps it round the* DIRECTOR*'s leg and immobilises him*) See here, Mr Director… I've taken an instant dislike to you, mainly because you're the spitting image of a friend of mine who's a rat-face just like you. So I warn you, if you show your face round here one more time, doing the Zorro bit, I'll come and pluck you, like a daisy, right down to the little yellow bit in the middle.

He pushes the DIRECTOR *away from him with such force as to send him pirouetting, in classic ballet style.*

DIRECTOR: (*Staggering, dizzily*) What is this man doing in this cage?

FIRST DOG CATCHER: (*Steadying him*) I'm sorry, but didn't the other Director tell you about the favour we're supposed to be doing for the Registry Office?

DIRECTOR: Ah, yes, he did. (*He goes over towards* LOFTY, *but stops at a respectful distance*) Be that as it may, you'd best be behaving yourself as befits an animal of your breed. (*He removes the bucket from his foot*)… A breed noted for its meek and docile temperament. Otherwise, I won't even wait for the statutory three days to pass. (*His voice changes tone*) I'll bang you into the gas chamber straight away, and that'll be that, understood?

Once again he contrives to stick his foot in the bucket, but does not notice.

LOFTY: (*With his head jammed between the bars, almost screaming*) Understand what? Oi! Daisy! What's all that stuff about not waiting three days... the gas chamber ... and that'll be that? We had an agreement that after three days you'd go ahead and put me down, but only for make-believe. (*To the two* DOG KEEPERS) Look lads, let's not joke with gas!

DIRECTOR: (*Waving his arms like the conductor of a military band*) I never agreed anything with anyone. My motto is, and always has been: seriousness and a respect for the law! If within three days nobody comes to take you off our hands, then you will be put down! In a country where nepotism and little favours are standard practice, the least we can do is to make sure that they don't creep into the running of our Dog Pound. And now step aside, because I want you to introduce me to the rest of the staff.

He contrives to jam his other foot in the other bucket, and sets off with a military gait, followed by the two DOG KEEPERS.

LOFTY: (*He is completely taken aback. He shakes the bars of his cage, but the door remains shut. Tearfully*) Mummy, mummy, they're all murderers here. (*He shouts over to the other cages*) Hey, spaniels, alsatians, mongrels, give us a hand! Let's organise a mass escape, because I really don't fancy ending up in a gas chamber. What have I done to deserve it? I'm no 'Man's Best Friend', me! Wake up! Kick up a row... ! Do something! (*He pauses for a moment, hoping that something is going to happen*) Well, look at that: not one of the bastards moved! Well, you know what I say: you disgust me, and it serves you right, because anyone who allows someone to dock their ears and tails, to slap them on the nose without uttering so much as a word, deserves to end up in the gas chamber! I'm really pleased! Ha, ha! You see how pleased I am – Ha, ha! (*He breaks down into sobs that sound like a dog's yelping. Meantime, re-enter the* CONJUROR. LOFTY *shouts out loud*) I don't want to die!

GENTLEMAN: (*The sound of* LOFTY's *voice makes him jump, frightened*) Oh, you horrible, ugly brute!

He walks off.

LOFTY: Excuse me, Sir, listen… (*He barks, then speaks, then barks. Since the* GENTLEMAN *pays no attention, he tries to attract his attention by miaowing. The* GENTLEMAN *comes back over to the cage*) I've got something to tell you…

The CONJUROR *looks at him for a moment, and then turns his back on him. Once again,* LOFTY *miaows. And once again, the* CONJUROR *does an about-turn.*

GENTLEMAN: What's the matter with you?

LOFTY: (*Pleading*) Sir, take me away from here. Save me. They've tricked me. They really are going to send me to the gas chamber… They're evil here… especially Daisy-Features there… Take me away from here… Pleeeease…

GENTLEMAN: (*Moved, in a paternal tone*) But my dear doggy friend, rest assured that I would be more than happy to. For years I have been looking for an animal like you, to replace my poor Garibaldi. But you've got rabies, and one can't mess around with rabies! Suppose you took it into your head to bite me… ?

LOFTY: (*Pleading with him, passionately*) But no, I haven't got anything… I'm completely healthy! I was just having a bit of fun with you. (*Enter one of the* DOG CATCHERS) Look, there's the Keeper. You ask him, because he knows what's going on. And then, when you know the truth, if you take me away from here, you'll never have cause to regret it. I'll be so well-behaved! I'll do everything you tell me: I'll eat my dogmeat, my crusts and my dog biscuits. I'll sit, I'll beg, I'll retrieve, and, if you want, I'll even piss up against trees. Just get me out of here!

He barks and whines. Other dogs take up the refrain.

GENTLEMAN: (*Turning to the* KEEPER) Listen, about that retriever dog…

The conversation between the two of them is submerged under the barking of dogs. It's feeding time. The KEEPER *is distributing bowls of dog food from cage to cage. As the* KEEPER *does his rounds, he nods his head affirmatively. He takes the money, and signs a piece of paper. Then he comes over to the cage and opens it. He puts a collar and muzzle on* LOFTY. *The* CONJUROR *takes his lead.*

GENTLEMAN: There you are. As from this moment, you are no longer a stray. You've got an owner. But I warn you, if you don't behave yourself as you promised, if you start playing up, I'll bring you straight back to the Dog Pound, alright?

LOFTY: Yes, yes, alright. But before we leave, would you let me play up just one last time? Just a little bit…

GENTLEMAN: Alright, as long as it's for the last time…

LOFTY: Thank you! (*He snatches the whip from the* KEEPER'*s hand, and disappears off stage right. After a moment, he reappears from stage left, preceded by the* DIRECTOR, *who is hopping along, trying to escape the lashing of* LOFTY'*s whip*) Let's have you, Mr Director! Jump to it! We've got to do away with all this nepotism, and little favours! Everyone needs a fair crack of the whip! We must respect the law, and there must be equality for all: dogs, men, cats … and Dog Pound Directors!

LOFTY *takes up a position like a circus trainer. He forces the three of them to get into line. Then, with a crack of the whip, he makes them come forward, stepping high, as if they are prancing horses. They pirouette, dance and gallop. The three actors' movements are accompanied by a rising crescendo of circus music.*

Blackout.

Scene Three

Scene: At the Conjuror's House

As the lights come up, enter the CONJUROR *from stage right, in a wheel chair, passing in front of the traverse curtain.*

GENTLEMAN: (*Shouting at the top of his voice*) Lofty! Lofty... ! Here, boy... ! You see, he won't answer! And he promised me that he was going to be obedient and obliging. He's trying to give me another heart attack... Imagine it – me, believing a dog's promises! And a mongrel retriever, into the bargain! (*He rolls his eyes to the skies*) Oh, Garibaldi, my Garibaldi – you were a *real* dog! (*He arranges the fingers of his left hand into the shape of a dog's head, and strokes them*) You are the only one who really loved me! I used to love the way you wagged your tail... But this one, never! Not only does he have no tail to wag, but doesn't even have the stub of a tail. And he's stubborn and lazy into the bargain, and he won't pay attention when you're trying to teach him the tricks of the trade. The few conjuring tricks that I *have* succeeded in teaching him have cost me my health. An attack of nerves has confined me to this wheelchair. And to think that I saved that mongrel's life! He'll be the death of me, and he knows it. He's been gone for half an hour now, just to get a newspaper! Lofty! Lofty! (*We hear* LOFTY *barking from off-stage*) I've told you a thousand times, I won't have you reading my newspaper! Imagine it – a dog, reading a newspaper, and in the street, at that! What on earth are people going to think? Come on, come in, and, *do* start behaving yourself!

LOFTY: (*He enters on all fours, still barking. He has a newspaper between his teeth. He is wearing a tartan woollen blanket around his middle, and a spotty knitted woollen suit covering the rest of his body. He comes over to the*

CONJUROR, *and gives him his newspaper*)There you are, your newspaper – all yours!

GENTLEMAN: And the bread, and the eggs, and the rest of the things that I sent you to buy... where are they?

LOFTY: They're in the newspaper.

GENTLEMAN: (*Unfolding the newspaper*) But there's nothing here!

LOFTY: What do you mean, nothing? But I was certain... I remember laying out the newspaper... (*He takes the newspaper from the* CONJUROR*'s hands, and opens it out in front of his owner, mimicking the actions of a conjuror*) And I said: 'Please, could you give me two eggs.' They gave me the two eggs (*He mimes the action*) I took the two eggs, and put them in the newspaper, and then folded it up. Are they there, or are they not? Shall we have a look?

GENTLEMAN: (*Holding his breath*) Yes.

LOFTY: (*He spreads out the newspaper, holds the top edge of it in his hand, passes his other hand behind the sheet, and pulls out two eggs*) Hey presto! There you have them – two eggs! And then I asked: 'Could I also have some bread, please.' So they gave me some bread, and I took it, and I put it under my newspaper. Shall we see if there's some bread there?

GENTLEMAN: Yes.

LOFTY: Hey presto! There's the bread! Then I said: 'Look, I'm tired of waiting round here. Will you please hurry up with the rest of the stuff so that I can get off home.' So they gave me the rest. I took it, and put it under the newspaper. Shall we see if it's there? Hey presto! And here's all the rest!

He pulls out a tray full of fruit, green vegetables, sausages and other foodstuffs. He puts the tray on the palm of his owner's hand. He raises his owner's other hand into the same position, as if he was a grocer's scales. He presses lightly on the palm of the other hand, and the two hands move up and down, alternately.

LOFTY: You see? The weight is correct, down to the last gramme! And you said that I was thick, and that I'm incapable of learning your tricks. Look: one, two, three, now you see it, and now you don't.

He contrives to make the whole caboodle vanish.

GENTLEMAN: (*Childishly enthusiastic*) Well done, that really deserves a prize. I'll give you...

LOFTY: (*Without stopping to draw breath*) Give me back my trousers!

GENTLEMAN: (*Craftily*) Ah yes – so's you can run away! No, no, no trousers... Since you've learnt your lesson so well, I'm going to take you to an old friend of mine who runs an equestrian circus. Ha, ha...! When he sees you doing the tricks that I've taught you... Ha, ha, ha...! I can't wait to see his face. (*Imitating his voice*) 'What? A conjuring dog?! I've never seen anything like that! Would you be willing to sell him? How much are you asking?' (*He takes up a determined stance, with arms akimbo*) 'I'm not selling!' 'Alright then, rent him: I'll give you a hundred thousand lire a month.' 'No!' 'A week, then!' 'No!' 'A day, then!' 'Alright, a hundred thousand lire a day!' And, wham, bam, shazam, cash on the nail! (*In high spirits, looking a bit crazy*) And you know what I'm going to do with all that money?

LOFTY: Set up a Hostel for Destitute Dogs?

GENTLEMAN: (*Laughing at him, cynically*) The dogs can go hang! I never could abide dogs, myself! I only like cats! And with that money, I shall buy myself hundreds and hundreds of cats, of every colour and every breed. Because I adore cats... (*He strokes the back of his left hand, as if it was a cat*) Miaow, miaow... Purr, purr...! What a shame that you're not a cat!

LOFTY: (*Like a little orphan*) But I'm very good at being a cat, I am. Don't you remember how I was miaowing in the Dog Pound? Miaow... Purrr! (*He finishes off his miaowing by spitting in the* GENTLEMAN's *face. Then, pursing his*

hands into claws, he lashes out with his paws) Pfuuut…
Pfuuut…

GENTLEMAN: But what's got into you… ! You're spitting in
my face… !

LOFTY: (*He gives a kick to the wheelchair, and sends the
cripple flying*) That's right, I'm spitting in your face,
because you are beneath contempt. You're a stinker, and
you're mad into the bargain! So it was all lies when you said
that you were a dog's best friend, and that you needed my
protection!

GENTLEMAN: (*Cowardly, terrified*) Come along, don't get
jealous! And I'll tell you the truth: I only buy cats so that I
can sell them again. (*Slily*) You have no idea the money that
can be made in the cat-trading game… Specially when
more than half of the leopard-skin coats in circulation are
in fact dyed cat furs!

LOFTY: (*He miaows and spits*) You double stinker! Not only
are you trying to skin *me*, but you want cat-skins into the
bargain… Damn you! Hiss… spit…

GENTLEMAN: (*Leaping from his wheelchair*) Hey, good
boy, down boy!

LOFTY: And, what's more, you can walk! You even stooped
so low as to pretend to be paralysed… just so's I would have
pity on you. And just because I'm tender-hearted, you
thought that I wouldn't leave you in the lurch… Damn you!

He gives the wheelchair another kick.

GENTLEMAN: (*Grabbing him by the collar*) Down, I told
you… Down! (*He forces him down onto his knees*) I'll show
you what happens to dogs who don't respect their
masters… ! Now I'm going to chain you up and give you a
thrashing!

LOFTY: And I'm going to bite you! Take that! (*He bites his
hand. The* CONJUROR *lets out a yell, and lets go*) And you
know what I'm going to tell you now? I really have got
rabies.

GENTLEMAN: No!

He looks at his hand, very alarmed.

LOFTY: Yes… I've got the worst, dirtiest, and most virulent kind of rabies – Arabic rabies! And now that I've bitten you, you've got it too. Good day.

GENTLEMAN: (*Tearful, in despair*) No, Lofty… ! Lofty… !

LOFTY: Down, boy! Down!

He exits, barking.

Blackout.

Scene Four

Scene: In a Railway Carriage

The curtain rises to reveal a section of a first-class railway carriage. Only two parts of the carriage are constructed in their entirety – one of the compartments, and a toilet, extreme stage right. As the curtain rises, we see a GENTLEMAN *in pyjamas, in the compartment, sleeping.* LOFTY, *still dressed in his woollen doggy coat, comes creeping down the train corridor. He notices a pair of folded trousers placed on the luggage rack. He snatches the trousers, and goes off to lock himself in the toilet. The* TRAIN GUARD *arrives, and gently and tactfully wakes the* GENTLEMAN.

TRAIN GUARD: Excuse me, Minister, we'll be arriving in a quarter of an hour…

He reaches out and shakes him.

MINISTER: (*Stretching and yawning*) Eh, ah, it's you… God, my back's all aches and pains.

TRAIN GUARD: Well yes, the bed… could have been more comfortable.

MINISTER: Too true. And this damned village where I'm

supposed to get off – even slow trains don't stop there. Why do I always have to get landed with tedious jobs like this?!

So saying, the MINISTER *fumbles in his toilet bag.*

TRAIN GUARD: Well, if you'll excuse me… (*He moves off down the corridor. He catches sight of* LOFTY, *who has by now put on the trousers, and who, at the sight of the* TRAIN GUARD, *beats a hasty retreat and goes back to hide in the toilet. The* TRAIN GUARD *becomes suspicious, and knocks on the door*) Can I see your ticket, please, sir… ! Sir! Are you feeling ill? Don't try and play fun and games with me! I warn you that if you don't come out at once, I shall open the door from outside. (*From his pocket, he pulls out a key. He puts it in the lock, and tries to open the door. But* LOFTY *hangs onto the door from inside. We hear a cracking noise. The* TRAIN GUARD *pulls out his T-key, and looks at it*) Damn! It's broken! I'll make you pay for this, if you don't come out at once. (*He pauses briefly*) Alright. I can wait. But I warn you, at the next stop, I'm going to call the carabinieri.

Inside the toilet, LOFTY *is still hanging on to the door handle. Meanwhile, in the compartment, the* MINISTER *is looking for his trousers.*

MINISTER: I could have sworn I left them on the luggage rack… (*Sticking his head out*) Guard! Where are my trousers?!

TRAIN GUARD: You called, sir?

MINISTER: Yes. I can't find my trousers. They've vanished.

TRAIN GUARD: (*Coming back down the corridor*) Impossible!

MINISTER: I remember perfectly well putting them up here. They must have stolen them while I was asleep. Maybe the thief thought he'd find my wallet in my trousers. Luckily, I put it in my suitcase.

TRAIN GUARD: Ah, just as well…

MINISTER: Just as well be damned! How am I supposed to get off the train without trousers?!

TRAIN GUARD: But haven't you got another pair in your suitcase?

MINISTER: Yes, I've got two pairs. But they're sports trousers, and I can hardly go to the opening ceremony wearing a black jacket with jodphurs or golfing trousers…

TRAIN GUARD: Hmmm… Looks like you've got problems! What do you suggest we do?

MINISTER: (*Eyeing the* TRAIN GUARD*'s black trousers*) Listen, why don't you give me yours? They're not exactly dress trousers, but at least they're black. What's more, we're both about the same height.

TRAIN GUARD: Ah yes, and I suppose I then travel in my underpants?

MINISTER: No, you can take one of my pairs of trousers. Take your pick. Go ahead and change, and in the meantime, I'm going to freshen up a bit.

TRAIN GUARD: Oh, alright…

MINISTER: Thank you. You are very kind. I shall remember you.

TRAIN GUARD: Oh, thank you, Minister. (*Exit the* MINISTER. *He goes down the corridor, and passes* LOFTY, *who has emerged from the toilet and still has the handle in his hand. He doesn't know where to hide it, and sticks it in his pocket. He passes swiftly in front of the compartment where the* TRAIN GUARD *has taken his trousers off. He has emptied his own trousers of his various tools of the trade, and is now struggling to open the suitcase. It won't open*) Damn! It's locked… !

He comes out of the compartment, and moves down the corridor, cautiously, scared of being seen in his underpants. He knocks on the door of the toilet on the left, into which LOFTY *has sneaked, to hide.*

TRAIN GUARD: Sir… ! Ah, there's nobody here. He must be in the other toilet. And the other fellow must have done a bunk. (*He goes and stands in front of the toilet where the* MINISTER *is now busily cleaning his teeth*) Minister...

MINISTER: Yes?

TRAIN GUARD: The suitcase is locked. If you tell me where you've put the keys... I thought they might have been in your jacket, but I didn't like to take the liberty.

MINISTER: (*Gargling, not thinking what he is saying*) No, they're not in the jacket. They're in the key pocket of my trousers...

TRAIN GUARD: Your trousers?

MINISTER: (*Realising what he has said, and almost choking on his gargle*) Pfui... ! They were in my trousers!! (*He coughs*) So what do we... ? Wait, I know a way of forcing the lock. Do you have a penknife?

He tries to open the door, but finds that it has no handle.

TRAIN GUARD: Yes, I've got a penknife.

He searches in his jacket pockets. Meantime LOFTY *returns to the* MINISTER's *compartment. He takes a stiff-fronted shirt from the luggage rack and puts it on. He also removes a jacket hanging from a hook by the window and puts it on. Only when he has put it on does he realise that it is a morning coat, with long tails.* LOFTY *takes them and flaps them, as if they are wings, fascinated, almost as if he expects to take off and fly.*

MINISTER: There's no handle on this door, though! Could you open the door for me, with your special key?

TRAIN GUARD: Well, the problem is, my key is broken. All because of that idiot earlier!

MINISTER: Well, think, man! Do something! I can't stay stuck in here. How far is it to my station?

TRAIN GUARD: I'm afraid we're almost there. (*He pulls out of his jacket pocket everything that could possibly be of use as a lever*) No, I'm afraid there's nothing we can do!

MINISTER: Well, hurry up. Call the other train guard. He's bound to have a key.

TRAIN GUARD: Yes, he has. But the problem is that he's at the other end of the train, and the door leading into the other carriage is locked, and in order to open it, I'm going to need the same key... In other words, the one that I've just broken. I'm afraid we're just going to have to wait till the next station.

MINISTER: I won't dream of it! I'm supposed to be getting off at the next stop... wearing trousers... and you must get me out of here at once! Pull the alarm cord, if you have to. Stop the train.

TRAIN GUARD: There's no point. It's already stopping, of its own accord. Excuse me, but I'm going to have to go back and put my trousers on.

MINISTER: No, you're not putting anything on! You gave me those trousers, and God help anyone who takes them from me!

Meantime, LOFTY *has finished dressing. He knots his tie and puts on his top hat.*

TRAIN GUARD: But I have to get off the train, to do my job! And anyway, if I don't get off, how am I supposed to get the key from my colleague?

The train comes to a halt.

MINISTER: Call him from the window.

LOFTY *prepares to get off. The* STATION MASTER *appears.* LOFTY *gets off, only to find himself sandwiched between two* CARABINIERI *in full uniform. Resigned, he makes as if to let himself be handcuffed. A* GENTLEMAN *with a tricolour sash around his waist comes forward to shake his hand. One of the* CARABINIERI *brings down his suitcase, and, taking the* TRAIN GUARD'*s trousers, wraps them in a newspaper, and passes them to the other* CARABINIERE.

TRAIN GUARD: (*Still glued to the toilet door*) But the other guard doesn't get off the train. It's not his job.

MINISTER: Well, do what you want, then. But I warn you that if you don't get me out of here in time, I am going to report you, and I shall have you sacked, and I shall put an end to your career!

TRAIN GUARD: (*He runs to the compartment. He finds it empty*) My trousers! Where's my trousers?

The group has exited, to the sound of a fanfare. The STATION MASTER *comes looking for the* TRAIN GUARD.

STATION MASTER: Guard! Hey, Guard...! Where are you?

TRAIN GUARD: (*Showing his face*) Here I am.

STATION MASTER: Well, don't you fellows get off the train any more? Who's going to blow the whistle for the train to leave?

TRAIN GUARD: I was looking for my trousers... But they've disappeared too, and I can hardly show myself like this.

He steps forward in his underpants.

STATION MASTER: Have you gone mad?!

TRAIN GUARD: I took them off for the Minister. He wouldn't take no for an answer! He wanted them, at any cost!

STATION MASTER: The Minister wanted your trousers?! What Minister?!

TRAIN GUARD: The one who's in the toilet.

STATION MASTER: But the Minister has just got off! There he is, going off with the Mayor and the others.

TRAIN GUARD: So in that case, who's this fellow?

STATION MASTER: How should I know? But this is complete madness – letting people snitch the trousers off you, and they're not even Government ministers!

TRAIN GUARD: Ah, now I realise who he is... It's the same

fellow that locked himself in before… So that's why he was
pretending that he couldn't get out. He was pretending to
be the Minister – but the real Minister went off with my
trousers, thinking that I had taken his. If I get my hands on
this one, I'll kill him. I'll throw him out of the window. No.
First I'll make him give me his trousers, and then I'll kill
him!

STATION MASTER: Throw him anywhere you want, but in
the meantime, can we get this train moving, because it's
running late already.

*He raises his green flag. We hear the sound of the steam
engine puffing into life, and we have the impression that the
train is leaving, because the* STATION MASTER *moves off
sideways across front-stage, to disappear into the wings.*

MINISTER: (*Shouting*) Stop! Stop! You mustn't let this train
leave! Let me off! Guard, open up!

TRAIN GUARD: (*Removing his jacket*) Don't worry, I'll open
up alright. But this time I'll batter the door down! I'll teach
you to play tricks with people who've got a job to do! Your
days as a minister are finished, Sunshine!

MINISTER: My days as a minister are finished? What do you
mean? Oh hell, the government must have fallen again!

Blackout.

*We hear marching-band music, which continues playing
softly as a musical backdrop for the scene that follows.*

Scene Five

Scene: At the Opening of a School

*The lights come up to show the traverse curtain closed.
On-stage we see* LOFTY, *in ceremonial dress, surrounded by
council officials and their wives. They are drinking a toast.
Everyone raises their glasses.*

ALL: Cheers! Your health!

MAYOR: (*One of the* COUNCIL OFFICIALS *is whispering in the* MAYOR's *ear. The* MAYOR *then turns to* LOFTY, *with a broad, mischievous grin*) Ah, Minister… We've arranged a special surprise for you… Your wife is here.

LOFTY: (*He splutters, sending out a spray of wine that he had in his mouth*) My wife?!

He coughs.

MAYOR: Ahaa! I knew you'd be stuck for words! You didn't expect that, eh?

LOFTY: No, I certainly didn't!

He continues coughing, banging the MAYOR *on the back.*

OFFICIAL: The lady told me you'd be surprised.

LOFTY: More than surprised. Amazed!

MAYOR: (*Man-to-man, winking*) The lady arrived last night, and she asked us to keep her presence secret from you until the time came to drink the toast. See if you can remember why…

LOFTY: Why? Let's see if I've forgotten correctly: why?

OFFICIAL: Because today is your wedding anniversary.

LOFTY: Well done! Spot on!

OFFICIAL: The lady was right, when she said you'd have forgotten.

LOFTY: (*With a chilly laugh*) Ah, yes, she was right. Ha, ha…

MAYOR: (*He moves over to the wings, stage right. He extends an arm, in the manner of a compere inviting a singer on-stage*) Come on, Madam, you can come in now. We've prepared him nicely. (LOFTY *closes his eyes, and when he opens them again he finds* ANGELA *standing in front of him*). Minister, Minister, your wife…

LOFTY: (*He takes a step backwards*) Angela!

ANGELA: (*She takes two steps forward*) Lofty!

LOFTY AND ANGELA: (*In unison*) What are you doing here?

MAYOR: (*Hail-fellow, hearty*) Now look at that – instead of being pleased… Really, Minister, don't look at her like that. Just think, the lady has come all this way, just to celebrate your wedding anniversary. It just shows how much she loves you! Come on, don't be angry with her. I shall leave you two lovebirds alone. But only for five minutes. No longer. They're waiting for us to go and lay the foundation stone.

He exits, followed by the COUNCIL OFFICIALS.

LOFTY: (*Holding his breath*) Are you really married to the Minister?

ANGELA: (*In a low voice, trying to allay his fears*) No, I'm only his girlfriend. I needed to see him, and I passed myself off as his wife. Just as well that he hasn't come. Just imagine the fuss he'd have kicked up. He's such a bore, a bigot. Just think – he forced me to wear this dress back-to-front, just because of the little low neckline… Look (*She turns round, and we see her bare back, plunging to the waistline*) Now, I ask you. Isn't that a bigot?

LOFTY: (*Delighted, egging her on, emphasising the 'tri'*) He's a tri-got!

ANGELA: (*Not getting the joke*) Just as well that he hasn't come! (*As if only now recognising him for who he is*) Oh, how lovely to see you, Lofty! How happy I am to have found you again! (*She notices his ceremonial dress*) But what are you doing, dressed like this? My, you've come a long way!

LOFTY: (*Modestly*) Well, I started out as a dog.

ANGELA: (*Aphoristic*) Well, one always has to start at the bottom… (*Returning to her previous breakneck pace*) Oh, but how lovely to see you, Lofty! How happy I am to have found you again! Let's hope that HE doesn't turn up and ruin everything!

LOFTY: (*He chuckles, confidently*) Don't worry – I think we've seen the last of him.

Every now and then a WAITER *crosses the stage, filling glasses.* LOFTY *takes and drinks several.*

ANGELA: How can you be so sure? Do you know him?

LOFTY: I should say I know him! How could I be here, otherwise?

ANGELA: Did he send you to stand in for him?

LOFTY: No, he doesn't know anything about it.

ANGELA: He's in trouble, eh?

LOFTY: Yes, a bit...

He laughs, in high spirits.

ANGELA: I knew that he'd end up like this. He thought he was cleverer than everyone, and you see! I always said that one of these days he'd get caught with his trousers down!

LOFTY: (*Waving his finger, almost hysterically*) He has, he has!! (*He laughs shrilly, and then suddenly comes down to earth again, gloomy*) But how have you ended up with him?

ANGELA: (*Turning away*) It was your fault.

LOFTY: (*Surprised, he pulls her round, to look her in the eye*) My fault?

ANGELA: Well, if you promise not to laugh, I'll tell you.

LOFTY: (*Reassuring*) I won't laugh.

ANGELA: (*She rattles off the following speech in a monotone, without stopping*) When you went away, you said: 'I'll see you', and I said: 'I'll see you' too. (*The* WAITER *passes with a tray full of glasses.* LOFTY *empties his glass, passes the glass to* ANGELA, *and takes another full glass*) But instead, day after day went by, and we didn't see each other at all. And since I was longing so much to see... You're not laughing, are you?

LOFTY: (*Moved*) You really wanted us to see each other?

ANGELA: (*As above*) Yes. I even went to the café to look for you. But they told me they hadn't seen you for ages. And so I came to see if I could find you in Rome.

LOFTY: (*After a brief pause*) To Rome? To see me?

ANGELA: (*Looking away*) To Rome. I went to all the ministries. I trailed all over the place… I saw masses of people. (*She pauses. She looks him in the eyes*) The only one I didn't see was you.

LOFTY: (*He beats his fist against the side of the stage*) Hell! Just imagine! If you'd come to the Municipal Dog Pound… Zap! (*He makes a gesture to indicate 'There I was'*)

ANGELA: In the Municipal Dog Pound?

LOFTY: (*Hurriedly, in throwaway style*) Yes. Municipal Dog Pound. Cage No. 12… Umm… it's a bit of a long story. Get on with yours… What about the Minister?

ANGELA: Alright. I'm getting there. One day I ran into somebody who was the spitting image of the Orthodox Priest…

LOFTY: (*Delighted, he stops her. He continues, using her tone of voice*) But instead it was the Police Inspector, who used to have a moustache.

ANGELA: (*Hurriedly, rattling on, as above*) No, he was the Minister. I say to him: 'Hi, how are you doing, Priest?' He turns it into a joke, and, just through that, because of that resemblance, we became friends. (*She pauses, and takes his hands in hers*) And what a stroke of luck, because look how it's brought us together.

LOFTY: Speaking of resemblances, these people round here, don't they remind you of someone?

ANGELA: Yes. They remind me of all those fellows in your gang… and the women remind me of my crowd.

LOFTY: (*Heaving a sigh of relief*) Phew – I'm glad that you think so too… I thought I was beginning to go silly in the head… This has been going on for ages… I keep running into the same old faces. The only trouble is, I never seem to run into *your* face.

ANGELA: Me too. How glad I am to have found you again, Lofty! (*The* WAITER *re-enters. Yet another glass for*

LOFTY) You look really good, dressed like a Minister. You look even loftier!

LOFTY: Yes, it suits me pretty well. (*By now he is pretty tipsy. He is unsteady on his feet*) I've never ever felt so good.

ANGELA: I can believe it, with the way you've gone up in the world! I can see that you've learned to walk without looking over your shoulder. You remember?

LOFTY: I remember, I remember. Only one thing I don't remember: what have I come here to do?

MAYOR: (*Who has come over to them as they are talking*) Oh, really, Minister... You're here to lay the foundation stone for our new school!

LOFTY: Ah, yes, the school.

MAYOR: (*With a servile laugh*) Your husband is such a joker! This way, please.

We hear the sound of a fanfare. The traverse curtain opens. We are in a building site, decked with bunting. There is scaffolding and concrete pillars. A tricolour ribbon held by two ladies runs across a good part of the stage. LOFTY, *visibly staggering, is led across to the ribbon. He is offered a pair of scissors on a cushion. He picks them up, casually, and shows them to the bystanders. He tries them out, cutting in half a feather from a lady's hat. Then he takes the ribbon. He cuts it, and holds on to the two cut ends.*

Then with an elegant gesture, he folds the ribbon up, and cuts it into many small pieces. He goes and puts the pieces into a top hat, which he removes from the head of one of the bystanders. Then he gives a magic wave, and from inside the top hat he pulls out a large number of small flags on sticks. He hands these round to the bystanders. They applaud, delightedly. The MAYOR *speaks, over the public address system.*

MAYOR: And now, Ladies and Gentlemen, before we come to the laying of the foundation stone for what is shortly to be our new school, I would like to ask the Minister to hand out the prizes to these teachers of ours, who have done so much…

Because the public address system is malfunctioning, only occasional words of his speech reach the audience. For the rest, all we see is the MAYOR's *mouth moving.*

MAYOR: …justice …of liberty …our country …glory …love …Italy…

The bystanders applaud. Once again the cushion arrives – this time bearing medals. LOFTY *takes one and pins it to the chest of the first gentleman pointed out to him. He embraces him, and moves on. He finds himself confronted with the ample bosom of a lady. He is embarrassed, and does not know where to pin the medal. Finally he decides. He turns the lady round, and pins the medal to her back. Then he embraces her, with increasing embarrassment. Every time he hands out a medal, everybody applauds.* LOFTY *reaches* ANGELA. *He looks at her. He looks at the cushion, but there are no medals left. He goes over to one of the previous recipients, and with a smile he excuses himself, removes the medal, goes back to* ANGELA, *and pins it on her. Then he embraces her. Then he has second thoughts. He signals to the* USHER *who brought in the cushion, asking him to come over. With two fingers, he tweaks his nose, and as if by magic pulls a medal out of it. He goes back to* ANGELA. *He pins it on her, and embraces her. He looks at her, deeply happy. He wants to embrace her again, but without a medal, he can't. He returns to the bearer of the cushion, and the whole scene is repeated: he pulls out a medal… pins it on her… embraces her… Once again, he returns to the cushion bearer, but this time the* USHER *stops him with a wave of his hand. The* USHER *pulls a medal out of his own nose, and then hands it to* LOFTY, *who goes and pins it to* ANGELA's *breast. Everyone applauds. The* MAYOR *comes over, and taps him on the shoulder. The* MAYOR *also receives a medal and an embrace.*

MAYOR: Thank you, Minister. Here is the parchment… Would you be so kind as to place it in the stone?

LOFTY: (*Having embraced Angela for the umpteenth time*)
The honour is all mine!

*He takes the parchment scroll, unrolls it, and shows it to the
audience. Then he rolls it up again, and tucks it down into
the foundation stone. He lights a match, and applies it to the
hole. There is a shower of sparks from fireworks. There
follow bangs and flashes from all sides. Trumpets play a
crazy fanfare. Everyone flees, terrified. LOFTY and
ANGELA are left alone. They carry on hugging each other.*

ANGELA: Oh, how lovely… It really is you, Lofty!

VOICES OFF STAGE: There's no point trying to run away…
I'm going to catch you…

*Enter the TRAIN GUARD, still in his underpants, pursued
by the MINISTER in his pyjamas. Both of them disappear
off backstage.*

ANGELA: (*She breaks away from LOFTY and runs off after
them*) Hey, Minister. Wait for me!

*Re-enter the TRAIN GUARD. LOFTY runs off, pursued
by the TRAIN GUARD, who has recognised him.*

Act Three
Scene One

Scene: A Bedroom

We are in an Empire-style bedroom, if possible with a full four-poster bed. A set of double doors leads in from the hallway, and there is another door leading to the bathroom. Stage right stands a divan and two armchairs. Stage left stands a screen, with a small desk next to it. The hall door opens. Enter the MAYOR, *who hands the key to* LOFTY *and leads him in.*

MAYOR: Please, come in. Here's your key... (LOFTY *puts it in his pocket*) Well, how do you like it?

LOFTY: (*Looking around*) Not bad at all. And this is the bed where you say Napoleon slept?

MAYOR: Yes, the man himself. You see, before it was turned into a hotel, this building was the headquarters of the Austrian governor.

LOFTY: It's amazing how many beds that Napoleon has slept in! If you believed everything they tell you wherever you go, you'd think he did nothing but sleep.

MAYOR: (*Openly adulatory*) Ha, ha! I'd never thought of that! You know, you're the funniest Minister that I've ever had the pleasure to meet.

LOFTY: (*Meaningfully, but without stressing the point*) Maybe because I'm not quite the Minister I appear to be... (*He flops onto the divan, which stands on the right-hand side of the room*) Excuse me if I sit down, but after all that running... I haven't run so much since I was a Retriever...

MAYOR: What?

LOFTY: (*Almost to himself*) Nothing, nothing... just remembering early days in the job...

MAYOR: (*Flatteringly*) Of course. But – forgive me if I keep on about it – you were really wonderful today – your idea about fireworks, your conjuring tricks! A minister who can conjure – I'd never have expected that.

LOFTY: Well, let me tell you, in our circles anything is possible. Some people do somersaults, others walk on ceilings, there are quick-change artists, people who jump through flaming hoops, vote-swallowers. Jugglers are quite commonplace – anyone can do it.

MAYOR: (*Laughing*) If only they could hear you.

LOFTY: (*Pointing to three suitcases on a little table*) Whose are those cases? I only stole... I beg your pardon, brought... one...

MAYOR: They're your wife's. The lady slept here last night.

LOFTY: In Napoleon's bed? A good job he's been gone for a while – or I'd have had my doubts! Well, let's hope that she's managed to get herself unhitched from that pest in the pyjamas...

MAYOR: I beg your pardon?

LOFTY: Eh... ah... No, I was just saying that I was a bit worried about Angela, about my wife... You see, in the confusion, I lost her, and since I can't find my pyjamas...

He pretends to rummage in the suitcase which he put on the bed when he came in.

MAYOR: Well, if that's all you need, I can give you a pair of mine. I live in this very building.

LOFTY: (*He takes the suitcase and puts it down on the desk in front of the screen*) Oh no, really... It's not worth it, just for a pair of pyjamas...

MAYOR: It's no big matter. After all, what you've done for us... By the way, I forgot the most important thing. Here you are.

He hands him an envelope.

LOFTY: What's that? Ah, I see. And to think that I never believed in all that stuff about bribing ministers… !

He chuckles. The MAYOR *laughs along with him.*

MAYOR: And you can carry on not believing in it, because this is not a bribe.

LOFTY: Oh no? What a shame!

MAYOR: What a splendid chap! Always ready for a joke…

LOFTY: (*Bitterly*) You said it.

MAYOR: (*Still adulatory*) But you wouldn't expect, with the reputation that you've got round here – you know, we're not completely cut off from news from Rome – we wouldn't have dreamed of insulting you like that…

LOFTY: (*Disappointed*) You wouldn't?

MAYOR: (*Missing the point*) This is the money that has been collected for the monument to Man's Best Friend.

LOFTY: (*Falsetto*) For what?! (*He gets up*) That name rings a bell!

MAYOR: Yes, our monument to Man's Best Friend, to his faithful dog. Don't you remember that we wrote to you asking if you could do something for us?

LOFTY: Yes, yes, now I remember: the monument to the faithful dog, to Man's Best Friend. Aaaaoooow…

He howls.

MAYOR: That's brilliant! You're a dog to a T!

LOFTY: (*Not at all amused*) That's quite enough of that, thank you. (*He points to the envelope*) How much is in there?

MAYOR: Nine million lire. Naturally, only two million are for the monument. The rest is for the new Dog Pound.

LOFTY: (*Pretending to be both interested and moved*) Why, are you going to build a Dog Pound?

MAYOR: Yes. You see, unfortunately, the old one was destroyed during the War, and you have no idea how many strays we have infesting our town.

LOFTY: (*Waxing rhetorical*) But now, with a splendid gas chamber... Uhuuuu... ! (*He makes a gesture, indicating elimination of dogs*) Zap! Death to the Stray, and a monument to the Faithful! (*He pats the Mayor on the back*) Well done – it was clever of you to think of coming to me.

MAYOR: (*Inordinately proud of himself*) You don't have to tell me; we know that our money is in good hands.

LOFTY: Lord, how right you are!

MAYOR: (*Pointing the way*) Please, this way.

LOFTY: Where are we going?

MAYOR: To get the pyjamas.

LOFTY: (*Striding out purposefully*) Ah yes, let's have the pyjamas too, while we're at it!

They exit, and re-lock the door. A few seconds pass, and we hear a key turning in the lock.

ANGELA: (*She enters, followed by the* MINISTER) Here we are, this is it. Look, look, what a lovely bed – all big and soft. (*She caresses him*) You know, I didn't sleep a wink all night. Every time I was about to fall asleep, I began to think that if I slept, I would lose the satisfaction of thinking that I was sleeping in such a beautiful bed. So I turned the light on, and splashed a bit of water in my face, and that way I stayed awake. I just lay there, thinking, happy as can be...

MINISTER: (*Giving her a look full of feeling*) I tell you, I have met some daffy people in my time, but nobody quite like you...

ANGELA: Listen who's talking! This is the man who goes round in his pyjamas, running after train guards in their underpants... When I think of the face on that hotel doorman when he saw you...

MINISTER: (*Annoyed, hysterical*) You can pack that up!

ANGELA: (*Mortified*) Yes, alright, I will... So this is the thanks I get for pulling you out of the mess you're in... If it wasn't for the fact that the Minister who came to replace you was a friend of mine, you would have seen…

MINISTER: (*Sarcastic, bombastic*) Do me a favour, your friend… ! If he was kind to you, you owe it only to the fact of that stupid idea of passing yourself off as my wife… (*He notices his suitcase*) My suitcase! Thank goodness – they've found it! (*He takes the suitcase and puts it on the bed*) And I wonder what on earth he must have thought of me, always assuming that he believed you…

ANGELA: (*She sits down on the divan. She gets up again. She sits in an armchair. She gets up again. She goes and sits on the little table, and here, finally, she feels comfortable*) Don't worry, I never told him that I was your wife. And as regards him being kind to me, he has always been kind to me… even before he got to the top. And if you really want to know, when we first met, he even asked me to marry him.

MINISTER: (*Searching in his suitcase*) Voilà!

He pulls out a dressing gown.

ANGELA: Well, not exactly to marry him… But he did ask me to be his girlfriend, and I, idiot that I was, said no… And then I came and said yes to you. God, I must have been out of my mind!

MINISTER: (*Sure of himself*) You've got plenty of time to change your mind, if you want.

ANGELA: (*Sadly, pensive*) But who knows if that's still what he wants. (*With a little smile*) You know, when he gave me those medals, it seemed like he did. (*Sad again*) But with the job that he's got now…

MINISTER: (*Mocking her*) He might have had second thoughts, and…

ANGELA: (*She misses the point of the irony. As if speaking to herself*) But no. I mean that, for as long as he was playing Rigoletto, we could have made a proper couple. But now…

MINISTER: (*Sparkling, effervescent*) What, what? You never told me that you were in opera… !

ANGELA: (*Replying in the same tone*) Oh didn't I? Well, that was where I learned to play the part of La Traviata!

MINISTER: (*Momentarily taken aback by the promptness of her response, he continues, in high spirits*) Listen to her! La Traviata!! If you'll excuse me, I'm going to take a bath… And in order to show me that you are not completely intolerable, please, sing me something. If nothing else, it'll stop me from falling asleep in the bath. I'm dog-tired. (ANGELA *does not appreciate the* MINISTER's *snub. He goes into the bathroom. She pulls faces, like a naughty child. The* MINISTER *speaks, from inside the bathroom*) Well, come on, say something. Tell me more about this great love of yours. Ha, ha! You know what I say? I say you've been imagining things. A Minister – he comes specially from Rome to replace me. He's called Lovely Weather. He's an ex-baritone. And what's more, he's in love with you… . Even a kid wouldn't have dreamed up something like that… Ha, ha! Minister Lovely Weather… I'd really like to meet him!

We hear water running in the bathroom.

ANGELA: (*She stands there, silent, for a moment. Then she has an idea. She goes to the hall door, and knocks on the inside. Then she begins play-acting, in a loud voice, in amateur dramatic style*) Who's there… ? What… ? Oh, it's you, Lovely… No, dear, don't come in, because I'm not alone… Go away. He's here, in the bathroom… You want to talk to me… ? Alright, then, come in. But only for a minute. (*She opens and shuts the door, slamming it several times. She walks across the room, stamping her feet*)

But darling, don't make such a noise, he'll hear us… What are you doing? (*She mimes a passionate embrace*) Heavens, what's got into you? You mustn't hold me like that! Let me go, Lovely, let me go! You want a kiss… ? No, I mustn't, he might hear us… (*She kisses her own hand*) No, don't… (*She gives herself a slap on the hand*) I'm sorry if I slapped you, but you really asked for it… (*Imitating a man's voice*) No, no, no… 'Yes'… (*She kisses her hand, and then slaps her arm; she continues repeating the action, until she makes a mistake, and ends up slapping herself*) Oh, no, stop it, Lofty, please… Now go away…

(*Imitating his voice*) 'Run away with me… !' I can't (*She turns to the bathroom, in the hope of seeing the* MINISTER *sticking his head out*) Leave me alone… You'll tear my dress… (*She makes a noise like cloth tearing*) Scrccch! There – you see – you've torn it… What? You'll buy me another one, in white? (*She goes over to the bathroom door. She raises her voice*) 'Yes.' A wedding dress… ? 'Yes… ' You want to marry me… ? (*She begins to get confused. She gets the voices wrong. She speaks in a baritone when she should be speaking with her own voice, and vice versa*) 'Yes'. Alright, yes, I will come with you… Wait for me downstairs. (*She realises the mistake, and corrects herself*) I'll get my stuff together, and I'll be down straight away. Goodbye, darling… 'Goodbye, darling'. (*She kisses her hand, and then gives herself another slap*) Oh, I'm sorry. Force of habit… Goodbye! (*She opens the door, and then shuts it again. At this moment, the* MINISTER *appears, and watches her, amused, as he dries his hair. She feigns surprise*) Ah, it's you!

MINISTER: (*Taking off her voice*) Yes, it's me.

ANGELA: (*Pretending to be embarrassed*) Um, it was the… the waiter… he got the wrong door…

MINISTER: The waiter… ? A waiter called Lovely?

ANGELA: (*Still playing out her part*) Oh, my God! So you heard everything?! But I swear, I didn't mean to… The door was open… I couldn't stop him coming in.

She opens the door, and behind this door we see the other door, the double door.

MINISTER: Yes, I know this door was open, but what about the other one?

ANGELA: (*She tries the door handle. The door is locked*) It's locked?!

MINISTER: (*Laughing out loud*) Ha, ha! That's right, it's locked. It's been locked all along. I locked it, and here's the key. So tell me, how did your Lovely get in? Through the keyhole? Ha, ha! Amazing what love can do! Anyway, my compliments, you played your part really well! Thanks for the entertainment. But now slow down, and stop playing around, because I've got to write a couple of letters, to post tomorrow morning. Go to bed, if you like, and turn the light out, because I'm going to stay up for a while. (*He goes behind the screen. He sits down at his desk. He switches on a table-lamp.* ANGELA *throws a shoe, which hits the screen. The* MINISTER *chuckles*) Darling, I think I heard someone knock. Could you go and open the door.

ANGELA: Very funny!

We hear a key moving in the lock. The hall door opens behind ANGELA. LOFTY *enters but does not see* ANGELA, *because she has bent down behind the bed, to get her shoe. Seeing him come in,* ANGELA *speaks in a whisper.*

ANGELA: Lovely! But how on earth did you get in?

LOFTY: (*Happy*) Angela, thank goodness you've come back. I thought you'd gone off with that other fellow.

ANGELA: (*Pushing him to the back of the stage*) Shut up. He's over there, behind the screen.

LOFTY: Is he asleep?

The MINISTER *chuckles, and shakes his head, thinking that* ANGELA *has started on a replay of the earlier scene.*

ANGELA: (*Still in a whisper*) No, he's writing a letter. But you mustn't stay, because he might hear us.

LOFTY: (*Also whispering*) No way! I'm not going away, unless you come along with me...

The MINISTER *breaks off writing. He cocks a curious ear for a moment, and then returns to his writing, with a knowing smile.*

ANGELA: (*She embraces* LOFTY, *full of emotion*) With you... ? Oh, Lovely, do you really mean it?

She gives him a kiss on the cheek.

LOFTY: (*Touching his cheek*) Angela, a kiss?!

He gives her a kiss in turn, and receives a slap in return.

ANGELA: Oh, I'm sorry... it's force of habit, and also because I'm all emotional... (LOFTY *gives her an enormous bear-hug*) No, no, don't hold me like that, you'll tear my dress... There, see, you've torn it...

LOFTY: I'll buy you a new one.

MINISTER: (*Still continuing to write, he imitates* LOFTY's *voice, thinking that it's still* ANGELA *who is playing the two parts*) And it will be all white!

ANGELA: Did you say all white?

LOFTY: No, I didn't say all white, but if you want it white, come along, I'll buy you a white dress...

ANGELA: But how are we going to get out?

LOFTY: The same way I got in: I had the key! (*He shows* ANGELA *the key*) Let's go.

ANGELA *takes her suitcase.* LOFTY *gives her a hand, and also carries off the* MINISTER's *suitcase, from where it was lying on the bed.*

ANGELA: What a shame that we can't take this lovely bed as well.

LOFTY: We'll save that for another time. For the moment, I'm satisfied just taking you...

They exit.

MINISTER: (*Happily humming the tune of the Wedding March*) Ta-rum-ta-tum... Ta-rum-ta-tum... (*He applauds*) Well done, well done! Have you finished the touching scene... ? Ha, ha... ! That'll do for now, though. This time you went over the top a bit, eh? (*He folds his letter, and puts it in an envelope*) The first time, it was pretty good, almost believable. But this time, you ruined it. You overdid it. I tell you, your imitation of a male voice, well, it was painful... Real ham stuff... And then, I ask you, I've hardly finished telling you that *I've* got the key to the main door, and you fall into the same trap again... So how did you get out this time? Under the doormat? Ha, ha...! (*He sticks his head round the screen*) Angela, where are you? ... Come on, don't go getting upset, come on out... You're in the bathroom, I know. Come on, don't tell me that you're angry... After all, you were joking too, eh? (*He opens the bathroom door*) No, she's not here. Where are you hiding? (*He looks under the bed*) Stop messing about, Angela!

The hall door opens. Enter the MAYOR.

MAYOR: (*He does not see the* MINISTER, *who is crouched down looking under the bed*) Minister, here are your pyjamas... Minister!

MINISTER: (*Getting up, lost in thought*) You were saying?

MAYOR: (*Surprised*) Excuse me, who are you?

MINISTER: (*Annoyed, pompous*) What do you mean, who am I...? I am... (*He looks round*) But how did you manage to get in?

MAYOR: (*As if it is self-evident*) Through the door. It was open...

MINISTER: It was open? (*He goes over to the door and opens it*) It's open!

MAYOR: (*Looking at him very suspiciously*) Would you mind telling me what you're doing in the Minister's bedroom?

MINISTER: (*Rolling his eyes*) But then, if it was unlocked, and it wasn't you who opened it...

MAYOR: (*Insistent, coming right up to him*) Would you mind answering my question? Who opened the door?

MINISTER: (*He flops into an armchair*) That's precisely what *I'd* like to know.

MAYOR: (*He thumps his fist down on the back of the armchair*) Right. That'll do! Where is the Minister?

MINISTER: (*Not moving*) Here I am. What do you want?

MAYOR: (*Thumping his fist on the armchair again*) Will you stop playing the fool! Where is the Minister?

MINISTER: (*He leaps to his feet. He points a threatening finger at him*) Leaving aside playing the fool, which minister are you talking about?

MAYOR: Why, the Minister Lovely Weather!

MINISTER: (*In half-strangled tones*) Lovely Weather?

MAYOR: (*Speaking rapidly, with feeling*) Yes. He's staying here with his wife... Although, as far as I can gather, she's actually his girlfriend... But what's it to do with you?

MINISTER: (*Stuck for words, speaking like a ventriloquist*) Minister Lovely Weather...? So he really does exist, then?

MAYOR: (*Spreading his arms*) Why, should he not exist...? It's a good thing that he does exist! He's the best minister that we've got. (*He stops abruptly, and changes tone*) So, where is he?

MINISTER: (*As if about to faint*) He's run off with my girlfriend... (*He suddenly realises that his suitcase has disappeared*) And with my suitcase, into the bargain.

MAYOR: (*Amused*) Ah! So she was your girlfriend...? I like it!

MINISTER: (*Shrilly, on the point of tears*) Without my trousers, yet again!

MAYOR: (*Chuckling*) Well, I'm glad, because I've taken a great dislike to you...

MINISTER: (*He looks at the* MAYOR, *and suddenly has an idea. He picks up the letter-opener knife from the desk, and holds it to his throat*) Off with your trousers! Remove your trousers!

MAYOR: (*Stuttering*) But, I say... What are you doing?

MINISTER: (*He gets behind the* MAYOR, *and puts a stranglehold on him, still brandishing the letter-opener*) Remove your trousers, otherwise...

MAYOR: Yes, yes, I'll take them off… I'll take them off… But for goodness sake, don't ruin me politically.

MINISTER: Huh! You make me laugh. Politically… ! Give me your trousers!

The MAYOR *removes his trousers. He gives them to the* MINISTER. *All of a sudden, enter the* TRAIN GUARD, *still in his underpants. He sees the trousers, snatches them up and runs off.*

TRAIN GUARD: About time too!

Blackout.

Musical interlude.

Scene Two

Scene: The Street Café again

The lights come up, and the traverse curtain has been drawn across. The actors are positioned front-stage, in the positions they occupied during Act One, in the scene preceding the wedding. The action picks up again precisely at the point at which LOFTY's *four friends were busying themselves trying to wake him.* LOFTY *is still on the floor. One of the* FRIENDS *stands over him, patting his face, and the other, the one who played the* ORTHODOX PRIEST, *is sitting at the table, just as he was at the relevant moment in Act One. The stage lights come up gradually. A series of muffled sounds indicate that* LOFTY *is about to wake up.*

ANGELA'S VOICE: (*As if disembodied*) You see, you see how those two are stuck for words?

LOFTY: (*Talking in his sleep*) Ha, ha! And look at the train guard running!

ANGELA: (*As above*) Come on, let's run too… Come on!

LOFTY: (*Still lying flat out. Moving his arms slowly, but with* *his eyes still closed*) Angela, wait for me… Angela, wait for me…

FIRST FRIEND: He's still dreaming!

DOCTOR: Here, throw a bit of water over him, that'll bring him round!

One of the FRIENDS *squirts a soda siphon in* LOFTY's *face.* LOFTY *gasps, opens his eyes, and looks around.*

LOFTY: Angela… Angela… Where's Angela?

He sits up. He continues staring at his FRIENDS, *dumbfounded.*

FIRST FRIEND: (*Still giving him a slap or two*) Oh, at last! About time! You've had a right old snore, there…

SECOND FRIEND: (*Passing his hand in front of* LOFTY's *eyes*) Hey! Wake up! You've given us a right fright… ! You sounded like you were in a fever, the way you were spouting on…

THIRD FRIEND: And you weren't just talking! Did you know you were being a dog too… ? Uhuuuu!

Everyone laughs.

LOFTY: (*Very sadly*) So it was all a dream, then… ?

DOCTOR: (*Extending a hand, to help him to get up*) Yes… And for a full fifteen minutes, at that. We were on the point of calling the ambulance for real…

LOFTY: (*He pushes the* FRIEND's *hand away from him, violently*) What a dirty, rotten, lousy thing… to happen… ! It was just a dream… ! Hey, but that doesn't count… It's too easy to end your stories just like that… When you don't know how to take it any further, you just say that everything was a dream, and that's that. (*Still sitting down, he gives a kick to the* FRIEND *playing the* DOCTOR) Dirty, rotten, stinking, stupid, miserable, deceitful… (*He pauses briefly*) …ugly, bastard Luck! But I might have known! Just seeing everyone with the same faces as you lot should have been enough to make me understand that it

was a dream! What dirty, poxy, lousy, bastard, evil…
(*Pausing again*) … STUPID LUCK!

Everyone laughs.

DOCTOR: Come on, Lofty, mind your language. Now we're
going to cheer you up a bit! While you've been lying there
flat on your back, we've been preparing you a lovely
surprise: guess who this gentleman is!

He steps to one side, moving the other FRIENDS *aside, and
reveals the newcomer.*

LOFTY: (*With a start, jumping to his feet*) Impossible! No, it
can't be!

FIRST FRIEND: No, no! It's not the pastry-cook. Calm
down…

LOFTY: I know. He's the Orthodox priest.

They all look at one another.

DOCTOR: That's right. But how do you know?

SECOND FRIEND: Maybe he heard us talking, while he was
asleep…

THIRD FRIEND: Don't be daft!

LOFTY: (*Going over to the* PRIEST. *In high spirits. Touches
him*) You're alive!

PRIEST: Why? Does that upset you?

LOFTY: Mr Priest, have my friends brought you here
specially for my wedding?

PRIEST: (*Playing his part again*) Yes, my son… But calm
down, and relax.

LOFTY: (*As if completely carried away*) Mr Priest, you're
splendid. You're a wonder! Mr Priest, you're a whizz! Oh,
brilliant!

He kisses his hands, and gives him hefty slaps on the back.

FOURTH FRIEND: (*Grabbing him by the arm, and trying to* *calm him down*) He's cracked… ! Hey, Lofty, what's got into you?

SECOND FRIEND: He's taken too many knocks – this time he really has flipped!

LOFTY: (*He breaks free, and raises his arms, ecstatically*) Shut up, lads. It's a replay… !

THIRD FRIEND: What's a replay?

LOFTY: (*Whispering, almost as if fearful of breaking a spell*) Haven't you understood yet? We're going back to the start… . It's like in the pictures, where they show you a bit from next week's film, and then they show you the whole film all over again…

They look at each other, worried.

FIRST FRIEND: He's gone completely round the twist…

LOFTY: (*He hugs the* PRIEST *again*) Only this time, it's not a film – it's real! (*He stops abruptly*) Just a minute. I suppose I haven't fallen asleep a second time? Excuse me.

He hits one of the FRIENDS *standing nearby.*

FIRST FRIEND: (*Obviously caught by surprise*) Ouch… ! Hey!

LOFTY: (*He takes his hand, and shakes it warmly*) Brilliant! I *am* awake… And if I'm awake, and if he's the priest who was there when I was sleeping, then, if we carry on with the show, then we'll get to the bit with Angela in…

DOCTOR: But who told you that her name's Angela?

LOFTY: She is called Angela, isn't she… ? (*Excited*) Excellent! Mr Priest, on with the show… !

PRIEST: (LOFTY *lifts him onto his shoulders*) Hey, what's got into you?

LOFTY: What do you mean, what's got into me?! I'm lifting up the bride's priest. Wasn't that what you told me? Forward march, lads, take me to my blonde… I swear, if she's the same one as before, I'll grab her, and I'll *never* let her go. (*They form up in procession, as previously*) Let's go. Sing!

They exit, singing in chorus:

'Clasp my wrist tightly…' etc.

Scene Three

Scene: A House in the Red Light District

We are in the girls' room. In the middle of the room, as in Act One, Scene Four, stand LOFTY *and* BLONDIE, *with their wrists bound together.* LOFTY *has his eyes blindfolded, and the* BRIDE *has her face completely covered with a veil. The* PRIEST *is reaching the end of his service.*

PRIEST: (*Intoning, almost nasal*) My blood will pass through your heart, and yours through mine, because we shall be one thing until the end of time.

EVERYONE: (*Including* BLONDIE, *in chorus*) Till death us do part.

LOFTY: (*Euphoric, in the major mode*) Yes, yes… That's her voice, just like before… God, I'm all trembling… I don't think I can carry on…

PRIEST: You are now man and wife. Unbind them, and let them see each other.

LOFTY: (*Electrified*) Yes, yes… Now we can see each other… Hurry up and take this blindfold off… (*Two* FRIENDS *help to unbind them*) Come on, get a move on… Wait, I want to be the one to lift her veil…

He lifts the blindfold from his eyes, and prepares to raise BLONDIE's *veil, but he holds back for a moment.*

LOFTY: It's her! It's her… !Tall and beautiful, just like the one before… ! And she's even got the same dress, and the same veil… (*His hands are trembling*) Hey, no, I can't go through with it… My fingers are twitching like I was playing a piano accordion… Will you take her veil off for me… ?

He points to the veil still covering BLONDIE's *face. Two of the* FRIENDS *reach forward.* BLONDIE *ducks away.*

BLONDIE: No, keep away. I'll take it off myself… Because otherwise, you're going to spoil my hair…

LOFTY: Come on, get a move on, because my eyes are almost popping out of my head… (BLONDIE *lifts her veil, and we see a face that looks like a puppet's face. A long nose, all bumpy; a thin mouth, not at all feminine; the eyes are hidden by a pair of pebble glasses; and incredibly hairy eyebrows, which virtually meet over her nose. Everyone laughs, trying in vain to hold back the laughter*) Noooo!

He is struck dumb.

DOCTOR: (*Pushing him towards* BLONDIE) Hey, is that all you have to say? What do you think of the nice little wife we've chosen you, eh?

LOFTY: (*Shouting*) You pigs! Bastards! Shit heads!

He grabs the first FRIEND *he can lay hands on, and makes as if to strangle him.*

DOCTOR: (*Trying to fight his way free*) No… Let go… Let go, idiot… !

FIRST FRIEND: (*Joining with the other* FRIENDS *to try and make him let go*) Sit down, and behave yourself!

SECOND FRIEND: (*He gives* LOFTY *a blow to the kidneys.* LOFTY *doubles up*) Well, how's that for gratitude! She's such a lovely kid, and he doesn't even want her…

THIRD FRIEND: (*He sends* LOFTY *sprawling across the table.* LOFTY *responds by kicking him in the stomach*) You've married her now, friend. There's no going back now…

FOURTH FRIEND: (*He jumps on* LOFTY, *grabs him by the scruff of the neck and sends him slamming against the wall, stage left*) Are you going to calm down?! I ask you! Fancy

making such a scene in front of your new wife… ! Come on,
apologise…

LOFTY: (*Panting, trying to pull himself together*) I'm sorry,
but don't think I'm picking on you… If you're not beautiful,
it's hardly your fault… My quarrel is with these sons of…
(*He pauses briefly*)Well, you're in the business, so you
know what I mean.

(*He moves front stage*) But most of all, my quarrel is with
those who organise our dreams. (*As if addressing himself to
the 'gods'*) I would really like to know whose job that is…
Who is it? The archangel Gabriel? …St Michael? …St
Raphael? …Who is it… ? (*He points them out, as if he can
actually see them suspended from the ceiling of the theatre*)

But I ask you, archangels: if what they told me as a boy is
true – that the heavenly Father has given this job to you –
then why do you have to come and take it out on me… ? Is
it fair? Two-timing dreams – I ask you!! Hey, nooo! I'm
going to start swearing now, swearing so much that you're
going to have to block your ears with corks! Because, if
we've now come to the point where we can't even trust our
dreams… (*Shouting*) then that's really the end… ! It's
rotten… It's the most lousy, stinking, rotten… (*His voice is
tense, as if in pain*) But, for God's sake, what do you take
me for: a pinball machine, where all you have to do is put
in your 100 lire, and then let off steam by banging it around
and shaking it about to your heart's content?

Everyone laughs. But without conviction.

PRIEST: (*In an attempt to break the ice*) Come on, lads, what's
come over you? Isn't anyone going to kiss the bride?

FIRST FRIEND: (*Euphoric, in high spirits*)Yes, yes. Let's kiss
the bride… But him first…

BLONDIE: (*With a violent wrench, she breaks free from the
Orthodox* PRIEST, *who is holding her by the shoulders*)
That's enough! Stop it! (*She takes off her glasses, her false
nose and her stick-on eyebrows. We see the open, pretty face
which we already know*) A joke's a joke, but I say that he's

right. This is turning into the rottenest of the rottenest, rottenest... I tell you, you lot are really disgusting! I ask you, is it right to go making a fool of a man like him, looking like he's got the DT's... He looks...

LOFTY: (*Up until now he has had his back to* BLONDIE. *He suddenly turns round. He staggers, sticks his head forward, and swallows hard*) Angela!

DOCTOR: (*Going to sit, lolling, on the table*) I ask you, what an idiot. She's gone and ruined everything. And now the silly cow with the stiletto heels starts moralising...

LOFTY: (*With his eyes half closed, he takes his face in his hands*) Angela, I'm asleep again. (*He goes towards the* DOCTOR) Excuse me.

He gives him a whack round the ear. The DOCTOR *hits him back, even harder.*

DOCTOR: Hey! Why pick on me?

LOFTY: Ooouch! (*He leans on a chair, dazed*) No, no... I really am awake. (*He goes back over to the* DOCTOR, *and gives him another blow, which sends him sprawling to the ground*) That's for the 'silly cow with the stiletto heels'...

BLONDIE: (*Going up to him*) Thank you...

LOFTY: (*Very tenderly*) Thank *you*... !

BLONDIE: You're right to make them respect you! You know what I think? I say that even if you do let them make a fool of you, you're better that all these idiots rolled into one... I'm sorry if I let myself get involved in their dirty tricks too... Because if I had known that you were so...

LOFTY: So what... ?

BLONDIE: Well... How can I put it? It seemed as if I already knew you...

LOFTY: (*Lost in admiration for her*) You do, you do! Sure, you know me... This is a continuous showing. Haven't you realised that yet?

SECOND FRIEND: (*Sincerely and affectionately, putting his* *hand on* LOFTY's *shoulder*) Hey, Lofty! Now that you've seen how she really is, you're not swearing any more, like before…

THIRD FRIEND: How could.he? He looks as if he's been struck dumb!

LOFTY: (*He spins round. Samson among the Philistines*) Will you stop that… ? Because otherwise I'll boot you all out of here… ! (*Then, to* BLONDIE, *as the gentle hero*) You see how I shut them up? (*All of them, in chorus, blow him a big raspberry.* LOFTY *ignores them*) Listen, I don't really want to see the whole film over again… Let's skip the boring bits… Anyway, I already know how the film ends… I know that your name is Angela, that your father knew everything about plants and poles… I'm your pole… Just say yes to me, and goodnight one and all…

BLONDIE: (*After a long silence*) Yes.

LOFTY: (*Surprised*) What?

BLONDIE: I said yes.

LOFTY: Yes, you agree… ? Noooo!

BLONDIE: Yes.

LOFTY: Whew! Wow!

PRIEST: Here, lads, this is getting a bit bloody sentimental… Let's have the violins, quick.

They all gather in a circle, miming a gypsy orchestra. All this, to the tune of 'Clasp my wrist tightly…' LOFTY *and* ANGELA *are by now oblivious. They continue talking and looking into each other's eyes as if they were alone in the room. The* FRIENDS *and* ANGELA'S GIRL FRIENDS *continue to imitate the sounds and actions of a violin ensemble, playing softly.*

LOFTY: But if you say yes immediately like that, without even a moment's hesitation, well then… (*He looks up to the ceiling*) Hey, archangels! I really must apologise for what I said before… In fact, I should have known that you really wouldn't have anything to do with tricks like this… I mean to say, an archangel, taking the mickey… ! I always knew that you don't play pinball… In fact, I've been really stupid to fall for it! But the trouble was, it was such a good dream… I tell you what, archangels, you organise some really good dreams! Even better than Hollywood…

BLONDIE: (*Sweetly*) Hey, Lofty, come down to earth a moment! Look, what are we going to do? We can hardly stay here all night with this rabble…

LOFTY: Correct. Either we kick them out, or we go off, ourselves. Let's take the train, and go… go… Come to think of it, what about money… ?

BLONDIE: Well, I've got a little…

She is about to go over to the cupboard, stage right.

LOFTY: (*Restraining her*) No… No… It's OK, I've got the envelope! (*He pats his jacket pocket*) Oh, how stupid! I *did* have it, but that was in the dream. (*He suddenly stops, with his hand on his inside pocket*) Hey, I don't believe it… ! (*He puts his hand into his jacket, and pulls out the envelope, in which we see a large number of 10,000 lire notes*) There it is!

Everyone looks on, in silence.

FIRST FRIEND: Mamma! There's millions there!

LOFTY: (*Turning and looking up to the ceiling again*) Hey, archangels, no, this is going a bit far now! What? Are you trying to embarrass me? Show me up? First you bring her back to me, and now millions of lire… Hey, no, I can't accept them…

The FRIENDS *too are now looking ceilingwards, in amazement.*

DOCTOR: (*Gasping, in a whisper*) Accept them, stupid… That's real money… !

THIRD FRIEND: (*Feeling the bank notes sticking out of the envelope*) Hey, Lofty, don't forget that I've always liked you, and I've always been your friend… !

EVERYONE: (*Reaching forward*) Me too, me too…

PRIEST: (*Pushing his way through*) Me too!

LOFTY: (*Meeting him face-to-face*) You! Why, I don't even know you...! In fact, you, with all that business about the gas chamber... you've got right up my nose... (*Everyone looks at the make-believe* PRIEST, *disparagingly*) No, nothing for anyone. (*He flings his arms wide, to get them all off his back*) Rather than give a single lira to any of you, I'm going to throw the money out of the window...

With three strides, he moves over to the window, back-stage. He opens it, and throws the envelope down.

FRIENDS: (*They run up, almost frantic*) What have you done, idiot...!?

DOCTOR: (*Looking out of the window*) What a stupid idiot! He's thrown the money in the canal...

PRIEST: (*Opening the door leading to the stairs, and rushing out*) Hurry up, come on down, maybe some of it landed on the road...

The FRIENDS *jostle each other, fighting to get through the door.*

WOMAN: Hey, let me through...

FIRST FRIEND: Get a move on, will you...

Everyone exits, down the stairs. LOFTY *and* ANGELA *are left, alone.*

LOFTY: Are you going down with them?

BLONDIE: (*In a low voice*) No.

LOFTY: (*Speaking slowly, slightly anxiously*) And now that I don't have a single lira left of all that wad, do you still want to stay with me?

BLONDIE: Well, I'm sorry you did it, and if you ask me, you're mad... But seeing that I've already made my mind up... yes, I'll stay with you...

She comes over to him, holding out her hand.

LOFTY: Ah well, in that case, I'll pull out the wad again! (*He

pulls out an envelope of money from his trouser pocket)
Hey presto… ! There you are. Check it, please…

He hands the money to BLONDIE.

BLONDIE: Hey! Wow… ! But how did you do that?!

LOFTY: It's a trick that *they* taught me. (*He points to the roof of the theatre. Then, shouting upwards, he says:*) Archangels, you're ace!

He takes ANGELA *by the hand, and the two of them run off, back stage.*

Musical interlude.

Curtain.

WATCH OUT FOR THE TILT!

The night is like a gi - ant um - ber - el - la full of holes.

Some - one's shot it full of drops of lime. Like a gi - ant

pin - ball game con - struct - ed for King Kong, The moon is like a

flash - ing 'Re - play' sign. And our ci - ty's like a gi - ant

pin - ball too. The girls are flip - per but - tons there to press.

Ea - sy does it or they'll go in - to a tilt!

a tempo
(Rocky)

Stea - dy there 'cos this game needs fin - esse. [Instrumental riff: Trumpet/Trombone (8 bars)]

Watch out for the tilt! Watch out for the tilt! A

red light is - n't my way, gimme a flash - ing bright green 're - play'

Watch out for the tilt! Watch out for the tilt! Its the

ba - sic rule of ev - ery game but few can keep it in the brain.

Watch out for the tilt! Watch out for the tilt! [Instrumental riff: Trumpet/Trombone (8 bars)]

We're the tough - est, we're the quick - est, we're the

great - est, we're the gang. We scare the rich by nick - ing their dogs and cats.

And when we've ter - ror - ised them, so they start to moan and whine We

WEDDING SONG

KINGS OF THE INK RUBBER STAMP

Moderato
(Tango – straight 4)

To glo-ri-fy Eg-yp-tians they

built a py-ra-mid, A sta-tue for King Da-vid, Charl-ton Hes-ton made El Cid. In

me-mory of Co-lum-bus A-me-ri-ca they named. Nel-son for his co-lumn he's

famed – we spit on them. Da Vin-ci has his paint-ing the Mo-na Li-sa And

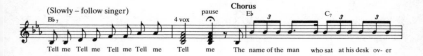

ev-en though its lean-ing there's the tower of Pi-sa. Each with his mon-u-ment they go

down in hi-sto-ry. Cle-o pat ra has her nee-dle, the house-maid her knee.

Tell me Tell me Tell me Tell me Tell me The name of the man who sat at his desk ov-er

aver-a-ges, fig-ures and norms Mul-ti-ply-ing, di-vid-ing, sub-tract-ing and add-ing,

Eif-fel has his tower. Gran-ny Smith has he

boot – we spit on them. Khy-ber has his pass in far off In -

bright up in the sky, the ma-gi had their star. Each with his mon-u-ment they go

down in his-to-ry. Ach-il-les has his heel and Earl Grey his tea. It

Solo Link
(Slowly – follow singer)

hurts us in our hearts there's no mon-u-ment for us. Who can name a fam-ous bu-reau-crat? We

Ad lib/Cadenza   **Chorus**

die a-non-y-mous! Tell me Tell me Tell me Tell me The name of the man who sat at his desk ov-er

aver-a-ges, fig-ures and norms Mul-ti-ply-ing, di-vid-ing, sub-tract-ing and add-ing,

check-ing the cen-sus forms. Let us sing of the deeds of the Lords of the rates and the

so-cial se-cu-ri-ty, Im-burs-ing, per-mitt-ing, dis-charg-ing and tax-ing, and

the man who sat at his desk ov - er

chron-ic - les, cat-a-logues, cal-en-dars, an - a-logues,

We broth-ers u - nite, for a sta - tue we fight, for our

work at the of - fice desk lamp. We stacked up the piles of red tape and files, Mul-ti-

ply-ing, di - vid-ing, sub-tract-ing and ad-ding, Im - burs-ing, per-mitt-ing, dis-charg-ing and ta-xing,

Chron-ic-les, cat-a-logues, cal-en-dars, an-a-logues! We're the Kings of the Ink Rub-ber Stamp. We're the

Kings of the Ink Rub-ber Stamp.

Eif-fel has his tower. Gran-ny Smith has her fruit, Not de - ny-ing Wel-ling-ton his

boot – we spit on them. Khy-ber has his pass in far off In - di - a. And

bright up in the sky, the ma - gi had their star. Each with his mon-u - ment they go

down in his-to-ry. Ach - il - les has his heel and Earl Grey his tea. It

Solo Link
(Slowly – follow singer)

hurts us in our hearts there's no mon-u-ment for us. Who can name a fam-ous bu-reau-crat? We

Ad lib/Cadenza   **Chorus**

die a - non-y-mous! Tell me Tell me Tell me Tell me The name of the man who sat at his desk ov-er

aver - a - ges, fig-ures and norms Mul - ti - ply-ing, di - vid-ing, sub-tract-ing and add-ing,

check-ing the cen - sus forms. Let us sing of the deeds of the Lords of the rates and the

so-cial se-cu - ri-ty. Im - burs-ing, per - mitt-ing, dis - charg-ing and tax - ing, and

add-ing on V. A. T. Tell me The name of the man who sat at his desk ov - er

re-cords, in - sur - ance and dole, Writ - ing chron-ic - les, cat-a-logues, cal-en-dars, an - a-logues,

ty - ing up ev - ery loop - hole. We broth-ers u - nite, for a sta - tue we fight, for our

work at the of - fice desk lamp. We stacked up the piles of red tape and files, Mul-ti-

ply-ing, di - vid-ing, sub-tract-ing and ad-ding, Im - burs-ing, per-mitt-ing, dis-charg-ing and ta-xing,

Chron-ic-les, cat-a-logues, cal-en-dars, an-a-logues! We're the Kings of the Ink Rub-ber Stamp. We're the

Kings of the Ink Rub-ber Stamp.